McCall's COOKING SCHOOL

McCall's COOKING SCHOOL

STEP-BY-STEP DIRECTIONS FOR MISTAKE-PROOF RECIPES

By Mary Eckley, Food Editor
and
Mary J. Norton, Associate Food Editor

Random House–McCall's–New York

Library of Congress Cataloging in Publication Data
Main entry under title:
McCall's cooking school.
1. Cookery.   I. McCall's magazine.
TX715.M122   641.5   76-14181
ISBN 0-394-40898-5

Manufactured in the United States of America
4   6   8   9   7   5

Contents

The best way to learn how to cook—be it a simple dish or something more complicated—is to watch an experienced chef at work. The next best thing to a live teacher is this book, based on the McCall's Cooking School.

For every recipe there are step-by-step word-and-picture instructions that show you, as well as tell you, exactly how the dish is made. From a series of four to eight color photographs, the home cook can see each part of the preparation and what the dish looks like at every stage. Accompanying each recipe is a full-page, full-color photograph of the finished product.

This unique cookbook is a natural for beginners and expert cooks alike. It is a boon for everyone who has wanted to try things like Chicken Salad in Aspic, or delicate pastries, or even Hollandaise Sauce, but has always been afraid of the complicated directions. And if you have ever attempted to follow deceptively simple soufflé instructions, for example, "gently fold egg whites into sauce," you know that getting it right is a hit-and-miss proposition unless you've actually seen the technique done by an expert.

The recipes cover every course from appetizer to dessert; they have been scaled to every budget; they take into account all sorts of occasions, from a simple, inexpensive family dinner to an elegant French buffet. Here you will find an Old-Fashioned American Potato Salad, an elaborate Breast of Veal Chaudfroid, and a traditional and foolproof favorite, Perfect Chocolate Cake. The whole range of good American cooking as well as specialties from French, Italian, Greek and other foreign cuisines are elaborately and beautifully described.

In addition, the experts of the McCall's test kitchens share with the reader new and clever techniques—for the pyramid-layering of apples in a perfect apple pie or for a chicken basted *under* the skin—all certain to enrich the repertoire and enhance the reputation of even the most accomplished cook. And to ensure absolute accuracy and success, these recipes have been checked and rechecked in McCall's famous test kitchen, so that even if you have never cooked before, by simply following the instructions, you cannot fail!

SOUPS AND SALADS

We think of it as French, but actually vichyssoise (pronounced veeshy-swaz) is American—or at least it's naturalized American. It was created at the old Ritz Carlton in New York by French chef Louis Diat, who took his mother's leek-and-potato soup, pureed it, then added cream and chives and served it chilled. Since then, it has become the single most popular cold soup in this country. It's easy and inexpensive to make this elegant dish in your own kitchen; the blender has simplified the process since Chef Diat's day.

AMERICA'S FAVORITE COLD SOUP

1 Trim leeks: Cut off roots and tips and most of the dark green, leaving some of the light green. Wash leeks thoroughly and drain. (If leeks are very sandy, it may be necessary to remove the outer leaves and wash and drain them again.)

2 Using a sharp knife, slice the leeks crosswise, about ¼ inch thick. This procedure should yield approximately 2 cups of leek slices. Have chopped onion ready; combine with sliced leeks. Melt butter or margarine in a 5-quart Dutch oven or kettle.

3 Sauté leeks and onion over medium heat until they are soft and golden—about 5 minutes. Stir occasionally with a wooden spoon. Be careful that leeks and onion do not brown; if they do, the soup, which should be creamy white, will be discolored.

4 Add potato, salt, pepper and chicken broth to leek mixture. Bring to boiling; reduce heat and simmer, covered, 45 minutes, or until potato is soft, almost mushy. This is important to insure that the soup will be smooth. Remove from heat.

5 Put potato-leek mixture into blender container, 2 cups at a time, and blend, at low speed, until mixture is smooth. Puree should measure 5 cups. In a small saucepan, heat milk until bubbles form around edge of pan. Remove saucepan from heat.

6 Add hot milk to potato-leek mixture; mix well with wire whisk. Refrigerate, covered, 6 hours or overnight. Before serving, gradually add light cream; mix well. Pour into 8 chilled soup cups; top with 1 tablespoon chives; surround with crushed ice.

VICHYSSOISE

1 lb leeks	**½ teaspoon salt**	**1 cup light cream, chilled**
½ cup chopped onion	**Dash white pepper**	
¼ cup butter or margarine	**2 cans (13¾-oz size)**	
1 lb potatoes (3 medium), pared, cut into ½-inch cubes (2 cups)	**clear chicken broth**	**½ cup snipped chives**
	2 cups milk	**Crushed ice**

Note: Vichyssoise is traditionally served very well chilled as a first course. It may also be served hot. If leeks are not available, substitute green onions. For extra seasoning, add a dash or two of nutmeg.

Gazpacho, a Spanish favorite, is a cold soup that's first cousin to a salad and even more refreshing. The base is ripe, fresh tomatoes and tomato juice pureed with other salad vegetables—cucumber, pimiento, onion and green pepper—and piquantly flavored with olive oil, vinegar and a touch of Tabasco. Serve it icy cold (recipes from prerefrigerator days call for cracked ice). On the side, serve small bowls of the vegetables used in the soup, chopped, along with crisp garlic croutons, for guests to add themselves. Step-by-step instructions, next page.

A CLASSIC SPANISH SOUP

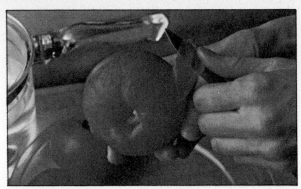

1 Prepare vegetables: To peel tomatoes, dip each tomato into boiling water for 1 minute; lift out with slotted utensil. Cut out stem end; peel off skin with paring knife. Or hold tomato on fork over heat just until skin splits, and carefully peel off skin with knife.

2 Cut cucumber into cubes. Cut onion in half. Wash green pepper; cut into quarters; remove seeds. In large bowl, combine two of the tomatoes, sliced, and half of the cucumber, onion and green pepper. Add pimiento and ½ cup tomato juice; toss to combine.

3 Put half of mixture at a time in electric blender. Blend, covered, at high speed 1 minute, to puree vegetables. Repeat with other half. Chop, separately, remaining tomato, cucumber, onion and green pepper. Refrigerate, covered, each in a small dish.

4 In large bowl, with wire whisk, mix pureed vegetables, remaining tomato juice, ⅓ cup olive oil, the vinegar, Tabasco, salt and black pepper. Refrigerate, covered, until very well chilled—3 hours or longer. Refrigerate six serving bowls and a tureen.

5 Cut bread into ¼-inch cubes. Rub inside of small skillet with garlic; reserve garlic. Add 2 tablespoons olive oil; heat over medium heat. Sauté bread cubes or the croutons in hot oil until crisp and golden. Drain well on paper towels and turn into small dish.

6 To serve, crush reserved garlic into chilled soup, mixing well with wire whisk. Ladle into chilled soup tureen. Sprinkle with chives. On tray, arrange reserved chopped vegetables and croutons to sprinkle over the top of each serving. Makes 6 servings.

GAZPACHO

3 medium tomatoes (1¾ lb)	⅓ cup olive oil	2 slices white bread
1 large cucumber, pared	⅓ cup red-wine vinegar	or ½ cup packaged croutons
1 large onion, peeled	¼ teaspoon Tabasco	2 cloves garlic, peeled
1 green pepper (8 oz)	1½ teaspoons salt	and split
1 canned pimiento, drained	⅛ teaspoon coarsely	2 tablespoons olive oil
2 cans (12-oz size) tomato juice	ground black pepper	½ cup chopped chives

MINESTRONE: A MEAL IN ITSELF

Minestrone means "thick soup" in Italian, and by the time you finish filling the pot with almost every kind of in-season vegetable plus pasta, that's exactly what you get. Ours is Genovese style, which means it's served with pesto sauce, a rich blend of basil and other herbs, garlic, Parmesan cheese, oil, butter and pine nuts or walnuts. For a complete meal add bread, fruit and cheese. Instructions, next page.

GEORGE RATKAI

6

1 Day before: In bowl, cover beans with cold water. Refrigerate, covered, overnight. Next day, drain. Turn chicken broth into a 1-quart measure; add water to make 1 quart. Pour into 8-quart kettle with 2 more quarts water, 2 teaspoons salt and the beans.

2 Bring to boiling; reduce heat; simmer, covered, 1 hour. Meanwhile, wash cabbage, and quarter; remove core with sharp knife; slice each quarter thinly. Pare carrots; slice on diagonal, ¼ inch thick. Pare potatoes; slice ½ inch thick; cut into ½-inch cubes.

3 Add to soup with canned tomatoes. Cover; cook ½ hour longer. Meanwhile, peel onions; cut in half; slice thinly. In ¼ cup hot oil in medium skillet, sauté onion, stirring, about 5 minutes. Remove from heat. Slice celery, on diagonal, ⅛ inch thick.

4 Wash zucchini; slice into rounds ¼ inch thick. Peel tomato: Hold tomato on fork over heat just to split skin; peel with knife. Slice ½ inch thick; cut into ½-inch cubes. Press 1 clove garlic. Add vegetables to onion with ½ teaspoon salt and the pepper.

5 Cook slowly, uncovered, stirring occasionally, 20 minutes. Add to bean mixture with ¼ cup parsley and spaghetti. Cook slowly, covered and stirring occasionally, 30 minutes. Make Pesto Sauce: Cream ingredients in bowl with spoon or with mortar and pestle.

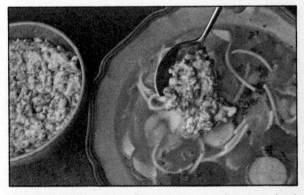

6 Blend butter with Parmesan, parsley, crushed garlic, basil and marjoram. Gradually add oil, beating constantly. Add pine nuts; mix well. Serve soup hot, topped with a spoonful of pesto sauce. In hot weather, serve soup cold, without pesto. Serves 10.

MINESTRONE WITH PESTO SAUCE

1 cup dried white Navy beans (Great Northern)
2 cans (10 ¾-oz size) condensed chicken broth
Salt
1 small head cabbage (1½ lb)
4 carrots (½ lb)
2 medium potatoes (¾ lb)
1 can (1 lb) Italian-style tomatoes

2 medium onions (½ lb)
¼ cup olive or salad oil
1 stalk celery
2 zucchini (½ lb)
1 large fresh tomato
1 clove garlic
¼ teaspoon pepper
¼ cup chopped parsley
1 cup broken-up thin spaghetti

PESTO SAUCE
¼ cup butter, softened
¼ cup grated Parmesan cheese
½ cup finely chopped parsley
1 clove garlic, crushed
1 teaspoon dried basil leaves
½ teaspoon dried marjoram leaves
¼ cup olive or salad oil
¼ cup chopped pine nuts or walnuts

A HEARTY OLD-COUNTRY SOUP

Nothing goes better on a cold midwinter evening than a bowl of thick, hearty, steaming soup. Here is something a little different—rich Russian borsch. In its native Ukraine, it's a hearty meat soup made with beets, onions, tomatoes and cabbage, topped with a dollop of sour cream. We serve it with its traditional partner, piroshki—small, meat-filled pastries. Instructions, next page.

8

1 Day before: In 8-quart kettle, place beef, marrow-bone, 1 tablespoon salt and 2 quarts water. Bring to boiling; reduce heat; simmer, covered, 1 hour. Add tomatoes, quartered onion, celery, parsley, black peppers and bay leaves; simmer, covered, 2 hours.

2 Remove from heat. Lift out beef. Discard marrow-bone. Strain soup in colander. (There should be 9 or 10 cups.) Return soup and beef to kettle. Add cabbage, carrot, chopped onion, 2 tablespoons dill, the vinegar, sugar and 1½ teaspoons salt; bring to boiling.

3 Reduce heat; simmer, covered, 30 minutes, or until beef and vegetables are tender. Refrigerate over-night. Next day, skim off fat. Remove beef; cut into 1-inch cubes; coarsely chop 1¼ cups for piroshki; return rest to soup, along with beets. Makes 3½ quarts.

4 Piroshki: Remove patty shells from package; let stand at room temperature 30 minutes to soften. Meanwhile, in hot butter in small skillet, sauté onion 2 minutes. Add 3 tablespoons sour cream, the chopped beef, dill, salt, pepper; mix well; reserve.

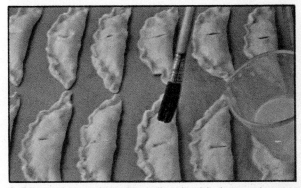

5 Preheat oven to 425F. On lightly floured pastry cloth, roll each patty shell to make oblong 8 by 5 inches; cut in half crosswise. Spread a rounded tablespoon of filling on half of each piece. Fold other half over filling; crimp edges to seal; cut slits in top.

6 Place on cookie sheet lined with heavy brown paper. Brush with egg yolk beaten with 1 tablespoon water. Bake 15 minutes, or until puffed and golden. Makes 12. Meanwhile, heat soup gently to boiling. Serve with sour cream, dill and the warm piroshki.

BORSCH WITH PIROSHKI

4 lb shin of beef	1½ cups thickly sliced, pared carrot (4 medium)	**PIROSHKI**
1 large marrowbone	1 cup chopped onion	1 pkg (10oz) frozen patty shells
Salt	2 tablespoons snipped fresh dill	2 tablespoons butter or margarine
1 can (1 lb) tomatoes, undrained	or 3 teaspoons dried dillweed	¼ cup coarsely chopped onion
1 medium onion, peeled, quartered	⅓ cup cider vinegar	3 tablespoons sour cream
1 stalk celery, cut up	2 tablespoons sugar	1¼ cups coarsely chopped,
3 parsley sprigs	1 can(1lb)julienne beets,undrained	cooked beef
10 whole black peppers	Dairy sour cream	½ teaspoon dried dillweed
2 bay leaves	Snipped fresh dill or dillweed	½ teaspoon salt, dash pepper
3 cups coarsely shredded cabbage(1lb)		1 egg yolk

Nothing adds to a buffet or barbecue like a spectacular salad— and Caesar salad is the king of them all. Crisp leaves of romaine lettuce; a dressing spicy with mustard, Worcestershire sauce and anchovies; and fresh croutons sautéed in oil and garlic combine for a salad that's almost a meal in itself. Then, like the original Caesar, a Tijuana restaurateur, toss it at the table with lemon juice, Parmesan and blue cheeses and—his secret and ours—a lightly coddled (not raw) egg.

HAIL, CAESAR! KING OF SALADS

1 Trim core from romaine. Separate into leaves, discarding wilted or discolored ones. Place in salad basket; rinse under cold, running water; shake well to remove excess moisture. (Or wash under cold running water; drain; dry on paper towels.)

2 Place romaine in plastic bag; store in vegetable crisper in refrigerator until crisp and cold—several hours or overnight. Several hours before serving, crush half clove garlic; combine with salad oil in jar with tight-fitting lid. Refrigerate at least 1 hour.

3 Heat 2 tablespoons oil-garlic mixture in medium skillet. Add bread cubes; sauté until brown all over. Set aside. To remaining oil-garlic mixture in jar, add salt, mustard, pepper, Worcestershire and chopped anchovies. Shake vigorously. Refrigerate.

4 In a small saucepan, bring 2-inch depth of water to boiling. Turn off heat. Carefully lower egg into water; let stand 1 minute; then lift out. Set aside to cool. Just before serving, rub inside of large wooden salad bowl with other half of garlic clove.

5 Discard the garlic. Cut out coarse ribs from large leaves of romaine. Tear in bite-size pieces into salad bowl. Shake dressing well, and pour over romaine. Sprinkle with both kinds of cheese. Toss until all romaine is coated with the salad dressing.

6 Break egg over center of salad. Pour lemon juice directly over egg; toss well. Sprinkle the sautéed bread cubes over the salad and quickly toss again. Garnish top with the whole anchovies, if desired, and serve salad at once. Makes 4 to 6 servings.

CAESAR SALAD

1 large head romaine
1 clove garlic, halved
½ cup salad oil (use corn, peanut or olive oil)
1 cup French-bread cubes (½ inch), crusts removed
¾ teaspoon salt

¼ teaspoon dry mustard
¼ teaspoon freshly ground black pepper
1½ teaspoons Worcestershire sauce
6 anchovy fillets, drained and chopped

1 egg
¼ cup crumbled blue cheese
2 tablespoons grated Parmesan cheese
Juice of ½ lemon (2 tablespoons)
6 whole anchovy fillets

Everybody loves potato salad—it's a summer staple. But why do some salads turn out to be delicious, while others are flat and tasteless? There's an art to making the real old-fashioned Sunday-picnic kind. And there's also a trick: The secret is to marinate the sliced potatoes in an oil-and-vinegar dressing while they're still warm. Then coat them with a well-seasoned salad dressing, and let the salad stand until the flavors blend. For perfect potato salad, use potatoes of the same size, so they'll cook more evenly. Be sure not to overcook them—they should be fork-tender.

McCALL'S COOKING SCHOOL

REAL OLD-FASHIONED POTATO SALAD

GEORGE RATKAI

1 In a 5-quart Dutch oven, pour just enough boiling water over unpeeled potatoes to cover; add salt. Bring to boiling; reduce heat; simmer, covered, until potatoes are fork-tender, not mushy—30 to 35 minutes. Drain, and let them cool 20 minutes.

2 Meanwhile, make marinade: In a 1-cup measure, combine marinade ingredients. (Or use ¾ cup bottled oil-and-vinegar dressing for marinade.) Peel warm potatoes; then slice, ¼ inch thick, into large bowl. Pour marinade over the still warm potatoes.

3 Toss gently to coat well. Refrigerate, covered, 2 hours, tossing potatoes several times. Potatoes will absorb marinade. Meanwhile, make boiled dressing (or you can use 1½ cups bottled mayonnaise or cooked salad dressing): In small, heavy saucepan,

4 stir flour with sugar and salt. With wire whisk, gradually stir in milk. Cook, stirring, over medium heat until mixture starts to boil. Boil 1 minute; remove from heat. Gradually stir the hot flour-milk mixture, a little at a time, into the beaten egg yolks

5 in small bowl. Pour back into saucepan. Add vinegar and prepared mustard. Cook, stirring constantly, until mixture starts to boil. Remove from heat. Stir in butter. Cool; then refrigerate, covered. One hour or more before serving, toss salad: Add

6 celery, radish, hard-cooked eggs, and dressing to potatoes. Toss gently; refrigerate, covered, until serving. Turn into a bowl lined with lettuce. Garnish with cucumber, eggs, radish roses, and onion. Makes 8 to 10 servings.

OLD-FASHIONED POTATO SALAD

Boiling water
3 lb unpared medium
potatoes (10), well scrubbed
1½ teaspoons salt

MARINADE
1½ teaspoons salt
1 teaspoon dry mustard
⅛ teaspoon pepper
Dash cayenne

¼ cup cider vinegar
½ cup salad oil
½ cup chopped green onion

BOILED DRESSING
1 tablespoon flour
2 tablespoons sugar, 1 teaspoon salt
1¼ cups milk
3 egg yolks, slightly beaten
¼ cup cider vinegar

1 tablespoon prepared mustard
2 tablespoons butter or
margarine

1 cup coarsely chopped celery
½ cup sliced radish
3 hard-cooked eggs, peeled and
coarsely chopped
Crisp lettuce; garnishes

BREADS

PIPING-HOT POTATO ROLLS

In this era of convenience foods, an entire generation might have grown up without ever tasting the delights of homemade rolls. Yet they're not hard to make, and it's easy to serve them piping hot for dinner if you prepare the dough in advance and have it waiting in the refrigerator. These rolls are especially delicious because they're made with mashed potato, which gives them extra moistness and a subtly different flavor. The same basic dough can be used to make all the shapes pictured here.

1 Prepare mashed potato as package label directs for ½ cup, omitting salt and butter. Pour warm water into a large bowl. (First rinse bowl in hot water.) If possible, check temperature of hot water with thermometer. The temperature should be no less than 105F and no more than 115F. Water

2 that is too hot will kill yeast; water that is too cold will slow down yeast action and rolls will not be as light. Sprinkle the yeast over water; add sugar and salt, stirring with wooden spoon until completely dissolved. Let stand a few minutes; the mixture will start to bubble slightly.

3 Add 2 eggs, the soft butter, warm mashed potato and 3 cups flour. With portable electric mixer at high speed, beat just until smooth. Add 2 cups flour, beating with wooden spoon until flour is incorporated in dough. Add remaining 1½ cups flour, mixing with hands until the dough is

4 smooth and stiff enough to leave side of bowl.(This takes place of kneading to develop the gluten in the flour.) Brush top of dough with 1 tablespoon melted butter; cover with waxed paper and dish towel. Let rise in refrigerator 2 hours, or until double in bulk. Remove from the refrigerator.

5 Punch down with fist. Cover; refrigerate. Dough can be refrigerated from one to three days, but punch it down once a day. About 2 hours before serving, remove dough from refrigerator; shape. For crescents (picture 7): Remove one third of dough from refrigerator. On lightly floured pastry

6 cloth, divide dough in half. With rolling pin covered with lightly floured stockinette, roll each half into a 10-inch circle. Brush with 1 tablespoon melted butter. Cut into 6 wedges. Starting at wide end, roll up each wedge toward the point. Place on a greased cookie sheet, 2 inches

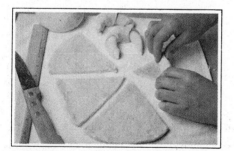

7 apart, point side down. Curl ends inward slightly. For figure eights and snails (picture 8): Remove one third of dough from refrigerator. On lightly floured surface, with palms, roll into a 12-inch rope. Divide into 12; roll each into a 12-inch strip. On greased cookie sheet, pinch ends together and twist

8 once into an 8. Snails: Press one end of a strip to greased cookie sheet; wind strip around itself; tuck other end underneath. Fan-tans (picture 9): Roll one third of dough into 15-by-8-inch rectangle. Spread with butter. With sharp knife, cut dough lengthwise into 5 (1½-inch) strips.

9 Stack strips; cut into 12. Place cut side up in greased, 2½-inch muffin-pan cups. To bake: Cover with towel; let rise in warm place (85F) until double in bulk—1 hour. Preheat oven to 400F. Brush with butter or with egg and seeds. Bake 12 minutes, or until golden. Serve warm. Makes 36.

REFRIGERATOR POTATO ROLLS

½ cup unseasoned warm
mashed potato or packaged
instant mashed potato
1½ cups warm water (105 to 115F)
2 pkg active dry yeast

½ cup sugar
1 tablespoon salt
2 eggs
½ cup butter or regular
margarine, softened

6½ cups unsifted all-purpose
flour
Melted butter, or 1 egg, beaten
with 2 tablespoons water
Poppy or sesame seed

BRIOCHE AND CRÊPES SUZETTE

1 Day ahead: If possible, check temperature of water with thermometer, or test by dropping a little water on inside of wrist; it should feel warm, not hot. Sprinkle yeast over water in large electric-mixer bowl; stir to dissolve. Add sugar and salt.

2 Stir to dissolve; add the butter, eggs and 2 cups flour. Beat at medium speed 4 minutes, occasionally scraping bowl and beaters with rubber scraper. Add remaining cup of flour. Beat at low speed 1 minute, or until smooth (dough will be soft).

3 Let rise in warm place (85F), covered with towel, free from drafts, until double in bulk—2 to 2½ hours. With rubber scraper, beat down dough. Refrigerate, covered with waxed paper and damp towel, overnight. Next day, grease 1½-quart brioche pan.

4 Cut off one sixth dough for cap. On lightly floured surface, form into ball, coating with flour. Turn out rest of dough onto lightly floured surface. Knead** dough until smooth—about 1 minute; shape into 5-inch round. Fit evenly into prepared pan.

5 Make 1½-inch-wide indentation in center. Insert ball of dough. Let rise in warm place (85F), covered with towel, free from drafts, until dough rises to top of pan—takes about 2½ hours. Preheat oven to 375F. Beat the egg yolk with 2 teaspoons water.

6 Gently brush surface of dough (do not let egg run between brioche and cap). Bake 20 minutes. Cover loosely with foil; bake 40 minutes, or until cake tester comes out clean. Cool 15 minutes. With small spatula, loosen from pan. Remove. Serve warm.

BRIOCHE

⅓ cup warm* water (105 to 115F)	1¼ teaspoons salt	3 cups sifted all-purpose flour (sift flour
1 pkg active dry yeast	⅔ cup butter, softened	before measuring)
3 tablespoons sugar	4 large eggs, at room temperature	1 egg yolk

*Water that is too hot will kill yeast; water too cold will retard action of yeast.
**To knead: With floured hands, fold dough toward you; then push it down and away from you with back of hand. Give dough a quarter turn; repeat as in Step 4.

(see page 127 for Crêpes Suzette recipe)

A fragrant loaf of homemade bread, hot from the oven, is a welcome addition to any meal. Our giant double ring of braided sesame-seed bread is spectacular enough to be the center of attention. Serve with lots of sweet butter and a hearty soup, followed by fruit and cheese for dessert. The important part of bread baking is getting the dough just right. Start by checking the date on the yeast package to be sure the yeast is still active. For best results, measure the temperature of the water in which you dissolve the yeast. It should be between 105 and 115 degrees Fahrenheit. If it's too hot, it will kill the yeast organism; if it's too cold, the yeast will take too long to work. Yeast dough needs lots of kneading and a warm, draft-free place to rise—place it over a bowl of warm water or in a cupboard or an oven with the pilot light on. For step-by-step directions, see the following page.

BRAID A RING
OF BREAD

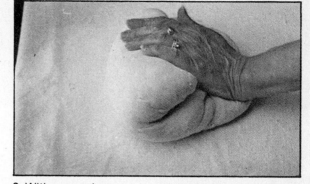

1 Into hot milk, stir sugar, salt, ½ cup butter. Cool to lukewarm. Sprinkle yeast over warm water (check temperature with thermometer) in electric-mixer bowl. Stir to dissolve. Stir in lukewarm milk mixture. Add 2 eggs, 3 cups flour; beat, at high speed, 2 minutes.

2 With a wooden spoon, gradually beat in 3½ cups flour; mix with hand until dough is stiff enough to leave side of bowl. Turn out on lightly-floured pastry cloth. Knead: Fold over; push away with palm of hand until smooth and elastic—about 10 minutes.

3 Place dough in a lightly-greased, large bowl. Turn the dough over to bring up greased side. Cover with towel; let dough rise in a warm place (85F), free from drafts, for about 1½ hours, or until the dough is double in bulk. Turn out on a lightly floured pastry cloth.

4 Divide dough in half; cut each half into thirds. Using palms of hands, roll each third into a 26-inch-long strip. Braid three strips; pinch ends together. On large, greased cookie sheet, form the braid into a ring (the center should be six inches in diameter).

5 Mix egg with 2 tablespoons water; use some to brush top of ring. Braid remaining strips; form into ring on top of first ring. Brush with 2 tablespoons melted butter. Cover with towel. Let rise in warm place, free from drafts, until double in bulk—about 1 hour.

6 Place rack in middle of oven. Preheat oven to 375F. Brush top of braid with rest of the egg mixture. Sprinkle with sesame seed. Bake 45 minutes, or until golden-brown. (If it's too brown after 25 minutes, cover loosely with foil.) Cool slightly on rack.

BRAIDED SESAME-SEED BREAD

1½ cups hot milk	2 pkg active dry yeast	1 egg
¼ cup sugar	½ cup warm water (105 to 115F)	2 tablespoons butter or
1 tablespoon salt	2 eggs	margarine, melted
½ cup butter or regular margarine	6½ cups unsifted all-purpose flour	2 tablespoons sesame or poppy seeds

A WREATH YOU CAN EAT

Make every day a holiday by starting off with a hot, buttery wreath of freshly baked Danish pastry. Ours has an especially delectable filling of almond paste. The secret is in the handling of the dough: Keep it cold and don't skimp on the number of rollings and foldings—every fold is one more delicate layer of scrumptious pastry.

1 In bowl, with wooden spoon beat butter and ¼ cup flour until smooth. Spread on waxed paper (on wet surface) to 12-by-8-inch rectangle. Refrigerate on cookie sheet. Heat milk slightly. Add sugar and salt; stir to dissolve. Cool to lukewarm.

2 Check temperature of water with thermometer. Pour into large bowl; sprinkle with yeast; stir to dissolve. Stir in milk mixture, egg and 3 cups flour; beat with wooden spoon until smooth. Mix in rest of flour with hand until dough leaves side of bowl.

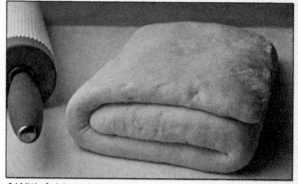

3 Refrigerate, covered, ½ hour. Turn out onto lightly floured pastry cloth; with covered rolling pin, roll into 16-by-12-inch rectangle. Place chilled butter mixture on half of dough; remove paper. Fold other half of dough over butter; pinch the edges to seal.

4 With fold at right, roll out from center to a 16-by-8-inch rectangle. From short side, fold dough into thirds, making three layers; seal edges; chill 1 hour. Repeat rolling and folding (if butter breaks through, brush with flour); seal edges; chill ½ hour.

5 Roll; fold again; seal edges; chill, wrapped in foil, 3 hours or overnight. Roll half of dough into a 22-by-8-inch strip. (Chill other half.) Cut into thirds lengthwise. Mix filling ingredients. Fill center of each strip with ⅓ cup; close edges over filling. Braid.

6 Form wreath, 6 inches across in center, on brown paper on cookie sheet; seal ends. Let rise in warm place 1 hour—until doubled. Preheat oven to 375F. Bake ½ hour. Cool slightly on rack. Mix sugar and milk; spread half over pastry. Decorate. Makes 2.

DANISH PASTRY WREATH

1½ cups butter or regular
margarine, softened
¼ cup unsifted all-purpose flour
¾ cup milk
⅓ cup granulated sugar
1 teaspoon salt
½ cup very warm water
(105-115F)

2 pkg active dry yeast
1 egg
3¾ cups unsifted all-purpose
flour
FILLING
1 can (8 oz) almond paste
(1 cup)
¾ cup crushed zwieback (8)

½ cup butter, melted
1 egg
½ teaspoon almond extract
2 cups unsifted
confectioners' sugar
3 to 4 tablespoons milk
Candied red cherries
Angelica bits

OLD-FASHIONED CHRISTMAS BREAD

When the March girls set out on a snowy Christmas morning to deliver their
own Christmas breakfast to a poor family down the street,
a loaf of bread went into the basket. Louisa May Alcott doesn't tell us, in
"Little Women," what kind of bread—but it may well have been a
fragrant fruit-filled loaf like the one pictured here. Surprise
your family with it on Christmas morning, served hot with plenty of butter.
(If breakfast is served late, there's time to make it that day—or
you can make it ahead and reheat in foil.) You might also serve it at a
holiday brunch.

1 Sprinkle yeast over warm water (if possible, check temperature with thermometer); stir to dissolve. In small saucepan, heat milk until bubbles form around edge. Pour over butter, sugar, and salt in large bowl; stir to melt butter. Cool to 115 to 105F. Add yeast,

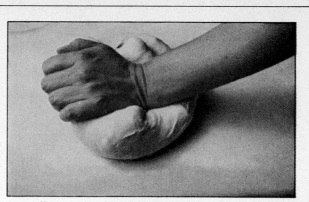

2 vanilla, egg, and 2½ cups flour. Blend; beat with wooden spoon until smooth. Add rest of flour; add last by hand. Mix until dough leaves side of bowl. Turn out on lightly floured pastry cloth. Roll dough over to coat with flour. Knead by folding toward you,

3 then pushing down and away from you with heel of hand. Knead until smooth and blisters form—5 minutes. Place in lightly greased bowl; turn greased side up. Cover with towel; let rise in warm place (85F), free from drafts, until double in bulk—40 to 50 minutes.

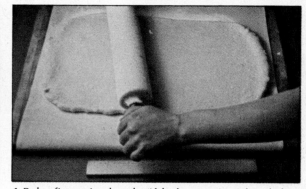

4 Poke finger in dough; if hole remains, dough has risen enough. To shape: Turn out on pastry cloth. Knead 10 times, until smooth. Roll into a rectangle 20 by 12 inches. Meanwhile, in medium bowl, combine filling ingredients; mix well. Grease a large

5 cookie sheet. Spread filling evenly over dough, leaving a 1-inch margin. Roll up lengthwise; place, seam side down, on cookie sheet. Shape horseshoe. Cover with towel; let rise in warm place (85F), free from drafts, until double in bulk—about 1 hour.

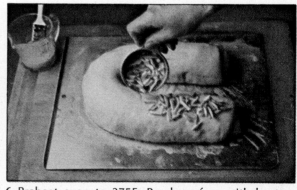

6 Preheat oven to 375F. Brush surface with beaten egg. Sprinkle with almonds. Bake 20 to 25 minutes, or until golden. (Rap bread with knuckle; it should sound hollow.) Remove from pan to wire rack; cover with towel; cool 30 minutes. Serve slightly warm.

OLD-FASHIONED CHRISTMAS BREAD

2 pkg active dry yeast	1 egg	1 cup dark raisins
¼ cup warm water (105 to 115F)	3½ cups unsifted all-purpose flour	½ cup diced candied orange peel, chopped
1 cup milk		½ cup diced citron, chopped
⅓ cup butter or regular margarine	**FILLING**	¼ cup slivered blanched almonds
¼ cup sugar	¼ cup sugar	
½ teaspoon salt	2 tablespoons butter or regular margarine, softened	**DECORATION**
1 teaspoon vanilla extract	½ teaspoon cinnamon	1 egg, beaten with 1 teaspoon water
		½ cup slivered blanched almonds

REAL OLD-FASHIONED JELLY DOUGHNUTS

You haven't tasted real doughnuts until you've tried the old-fashioned homemade kind with strawberry- or currant-jam centers and the incredible lightness that comes only from yeast-raised dough. Getting them just right requires care. The water in which you dissolve the yeast and the fat in which you fry the doughnuts must be exactly the right temperature—always use a thermometer. Take one bite and you'll know they're worth the trouble. Step-by-step directions, next page.

GEORGE RATKAI

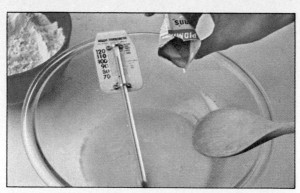

1 Heat milk in small pan until bubbles form around edge of pan; remove from heat. Add ⅓ cup sugar, salt and butter; stir to melt. Cool to lukewarm. In large bowl, sprinkle yeast over warm water (if possible, check temperature of water with a thermometer).

2 Stir yeast until dissolved. Add milk mixture, egg yolks and 2 cups flour. With portable electric mixer, at medium speed, beat until smooth—about 2 minutes. With wooden spoon, beat in remaining flour; beat until smooth. Dough will be soft.

3 Cover with towel; let rise in warm place (85F), free from drafts, until double in bulk—about 1½ hours. Punch down dough. Turn out onto lightly floured pastry cloth; turn over to coat with flour. Knead ten times, or until dough is smooth. Divide dough in half.

4 Roll out half of dough to ¼-inch thickness. Cut into 12 (3-inch size) rounds. Place 1 teaspoon jam in center of half of rounds; brush edge with egg white. Top with rest of rounds; press edges to seal. Place on floured cookie sheet. Repeat with rest of dough.

5 Cover with towel; let rise until double in bulk—about 1 hour. Meanwhile, in deep-fat fryer or heavy skillet, slowly heat oil (2 inches deep) to 350F on deep-frying thermometer. Gently drop the doughnuts, top side down, three at a time, into the hot oil.

6 Fry, turning as they rise to surface, turning again, until golden-brown—4 minutes in all. (Open one to test doneness; fry longer if needed.) Lift out with slotted utensil, draining slightly. Place on paper towels to drain. Dust with sugar while warm. Makes 14.

JELLY DOUGHNUTS

½ cup milk	½ cup warm water	Raspberry, currant or
⅓ cup sugar	(105 to 115F)	strawberry jam or jelly
1 teaspoon salt	3 egg yolks	Egg white
⅓ cup butter	3¾ cups sifted*	Salad oil for deep-frying
2 pkg active dry yeast	all-purpose flour	Sugar

***Sift before measuring.**

DOUGHNUTS WITH A FRENCH TWIST

French crullers and beignets (which are simply crullers made in round balls instead of ring shapes) might be described as doughnuts with a French connection. They're made with "pâte à chou"—the sweet pastry that is used to make cream puffs. When fried in hot deep fat (the temperature is important; use a thermometer) they expand to become light, airy and golden. They're at their best when freshly made; just serve plain, with a sprinkling of sugar, along with coffee. Or they can make the basis for a spectacular dessert with apricot sauce and whipped cream.

1 Make crullers: With shortening, grease one side of foil circles very well. In heavy, 2½-quart saucepan, combine sugar, salt, butter and 1 cup water. Bring to boiling; butter will melt. Remove from heat. Quickly add flour all at once; beat with wooden spoon until

2 flour is moistened. Cook over medium heat, beating vigorously until dough forms ball and leaves side of pan. Remove from heat. Add eggs, one at a time, beating with electric mixer at medium speed after each addition. Continue beating until the mixture is

3 smooth, shiny and satiny and forms strands that break apart. It should hold its shape when beater is slowly raised. Beat in vanilla. To make crullers, turn mixture into a large pastry bag with a number-6 star tip. Press mixture onto greased foil to form circles

4 about 3¼ inches in diameter, overlapping ends of circles slightly. Let stand 20 minutes. In electric skillet or large, heavy skillet, slowly heat oil (1½ to 2 inches) to 350F on deep-frying thermometer. Place crullers, including the foil, in hot oil, four at a time.

5 Turn each as it rises to top. Lift out foil. Fry about 10 minutes, or until golden, turning several times. Lift out with slotted spoon. Drain on paper towels; remove to wire rack. Serve warm, sprinkled with confectioners' sugar. Makes 14. For beignets, drop

6 batter by rounded tablespoonfuls into hot oil, six at a time. Fry about 7 minutes, or until golden, turning several times. Lift out; drain. Keep warm in oven. Melt preserves with lemon juice; strain; add kirsch. Serve with warm beignets and cream. Makes 24.

FRENCH CRULLERS AND BEIGNETS

Shortening
14 (3½-inch) foil circles

2 tablespoons granulated sugar
½ teaspoon salt
¼ cup butter or regular
margarine

1¼ cups sifted
all-purpose flour
4 eggs
1 teaspoon vanilla extract
Salad oil or shortening
for frying
Confectioners' sugar

APRICOT SAUCE
1 jar (12 oz) apricot
preserves
2 tablespoons lemon juice
½ tablespoon kirsch

Sweetened whipped cream

MAIN COURSES

This cool, shimmering, molded chicken in aspic, served with hot rolls, salad and dessert, is perfect for a luncheon party, but it would also make a simple but festive dinner for one of the warm nights to come. And it could of course star at any buffet. The best part is that it's much easier to make than it looks. Cooked chicken slices line a bowl, which is filled with a rich aspic made from chicken stock and flavored with lemon, herbs, spices and chopped vegetables. There's a trick to insuring that the cucumber slices and capers will be symmetrically and neatly arranged. Instead of placing them inside the mold, they're put on after the dish has been chilled and unmolded. Then it is quickly glazed with wine-flavored aspic and rechilled. Garnish with tomato and pepper slices and lettuce, and serve with a curry-flavored mayonnaise.

SALAD SUPREME: CHICKEN IN ASPIC

1 Rinse chicken well under cold water. In 6-quart Dutch oven, place carrots and next nine ingredients. Add chicken, breast side down. Add 4 cups water; bring to boiling. Reduce heat; simmer gently, covered, 1 hour. Turn chicken; simmer 1 hour, or until just tender, not soft. Remove chicken from broth; let cool. Strain broth

2 through strainer lined with cheesecloth; discard vegetables; skim off fat. Measure broth. Boil, uncovered, to reduce to 4 cups. Make aspic: Sprinkle 2 envelopes gelatine over ¼ cup cold water; let stand to soften. Add to hot broth; bring to boiling, stirring to dissolve. Add ⅓ cup lemon juice. Pour ½ cup gelatine mixture into

3 a 2-quart mold or bowl; refrigerate until set—1 hour. Turn rest into medium bowl set in bowl of ice cubes; let stand, stirring occasionally, until consistency of unbeaten egg white—25 minutes. Meanwhile, slice breast of chicken thinly. Coat slices well with thickened gelatine; overlap around inside of mold, lining completely.

4 Remove chicken from bones; cut into ½-inch cubes with rest of sliced chicken (4 cups). Mix with chopped vegetables and rest of gelatine mixture. Turn into center of mold. Refrigerate, covered with waxed paper, until firm—overnight. To unmold: Quickly dip bottom of mold into hot water; run spatula around edge; invert on

5 rack set on tray or serving dish; refrigerate. Make glaze: Sprinkle gelatine over ¼ cup cold water in small saucepan; let stand 5 minutes to soften. Add wine; stir over low heat to dissolve gelatine. Set pan in ice water; let stand, stirring occasionally, until thickened—15 minutes. Arrange cucumber around bottom of mold; place 7

6 slices on top with capers and pimiento to form flower, as pictured. Spoon half of glaze over top, covering completely. Refrigerate ½ hour. Reheat rest of glaze; cool; spoon over top. Refrigerate. Garnish with the greens, tomato and green pepper. Serve with mayonnaise mixed with lemon juice and curry powder. Serves 10.

CHICKEN SALAD IN ASPIC

5-lb ready-to-cook roasting or stewing chicken	4 slices lemon	**GLAZE**
3 carrots, pared and halved	1 can (10¾ oz) condensed chicken broth, undiluted	1 env unflavored gelatine
1 stalk celery, cut up		1 cup white wine
1 large onion, peeled and sliced	**ASPIC**	
2 sprigs parsley	2 env unflavored gelatine	Thin cucumber slices, halved
6 whole cloves	⅓ cup lemon juice	Capers, pimiento, greens
10 whole black peppers	⅓ cup chopped green pepper	Tomato and green-pepper slices
2 bay leaves	⅓ cup finely chopped pimiento	1 cup mayonnaise
1 tablespoon salt	⅓ cup finely chopped celery	2 tablespoons lemon juice
		1½ teaspoons curry powder

No broilers or fryers here—only a plump, old-fashioned roaster, with plenty of tender meat on its bones, will do for this luxury version of a Sunday roast chicken. Stuffed with seasoned bread cubes and chicken liver for richness, it is served with giblet gravy made with extra chicken broth and a touch of celery. But the real secret of this dish is in the roasting method. The herbed butter that is stuffed under the skin of the breast guarantees tenderness and lets the flavors of lemon, parsley, and onion permeate the meat while the bird is cooking. Herb butter: In a small bowl, using a fork, beat ⅓ cup butter or margarine, softened to room temperature, with 2 teaspoons lemon juice, 2 tablespoons chopped parsley, 1 tablespoon chopped green onion, ½ teaspoon salt, and ⅛ teaspoon pepper.

McCall's Cooking School

A CHICKEN TRICK: ROAST IT WITH BUTTER UNDER THE SKIN

1 Preheat oven to 350F. Remove giblets from chicken. Set aside liver for stuffing. Wash chicken inside and out with cold running water, and pat dry with paper towels.

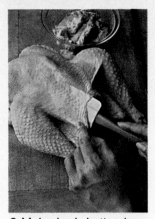

2 Make herb butter (see previous page). With a rubber scraper, carefully loosen the skin from either side of the chicken breast, taking care not to break through the skin.

3 Carefully spread half of herb butter over breast meat under skin on each side, using metal spatula or rubber scraper. Cautiously push the herb butter in as far as it will go.

4 Make stuffing (ingredients at right): In ½ cup hot butter, sauté celery, onion, liver until celery is golden. Remove from heat; toss with rest of ingredients in large bowl.

5 Stuff neck, body cavities. Bring neck skin over back. Tuck wings under. Close body cavity with poultry pin. Loop twine around pin; crisscross over opening, under

6 opposite leg, up around legs; bring together. Bring twine under opposite leg, up under wings; tie over back. Roast on rack in roasting pan, uncovered, 1¾ to 2 hours.

7 Baste occasionally with drippings. When done, leg should move up and down easily and flesh feel soft. Remove pins and twine; let stand 15 minutes before carving.

8 Make gravy: In saucepan, mix all ingredients (right) but flour. Add ¾ cup water; simmer, covered, 1½ hours. Strain; add water to make 2 cups. Chop giblets fine.

9 Pour off pan drippings. Return ¼ cup to pan; stir in flour (not on heat) until smooth. Add broth; bring to boil, stirring. Add giblets. Reduce heat; simmer 1 minute. Season.

ROAST CHICKEN WITH HERBS

1 whole, ready-to-cook roasting chicken (about 5 lb)

STUFFING
½ cup butter or margarine
½ cup chopped celery
½ cup chopped green onion
1 chicken liver, chopped
4 cups day-old white-bread cubes, or 1 pkg (8 oz) seasoned bread cubes
2 tablespoons chopped parsley
½ teaspoon dried thyme leaves
½ teaspoon salt
⅛ teaspoon pepper

GIBLET GRAVY
Giblets and neck
1 onion, peeled and halved
Celery tops from 1 stalk
2 whole black peppercorns
½ teaspoon salt
1 can (10½ oz) condensed chicken broth, undiluted
¼ cup flour

CHICKEN WITH A RUSSIAN ACCENT

Created in the Russia of the high-living Czars, Chicken Kiev is the most elegant of chicken dishes. Chicken breasts, first boned and skinned, are pounded thin, then wrapped around pats of seasoned frozen butter, coated with egg and crumbs, and deep-fried until golden. By the time chicken is done, butter is just melted and will gush from the chicken breast when you cut into it. Serve with fresh asparagus and fluffy white rice. Chicken Kiev can be cooked ahead and frozen: Cool, wrap in freezer-wrap, and freeze. To serve, unwrap packets, but do not defrost. Bake, uncovered, 35 minutes in 350F oven.

1 In small bowl, with rubber scraper, thoroughly mix butter, parsley, tarragon, garlic, salt, and pepper. On foil, shape into 6-inch square. Freeze until firm—about 40 minutes.

2 Meanwhile, wash chicken; dry well on paper towels. Using a small sharp knife, carefully remove skin. Cut each breast in half. To flatten chicken, place each half, smooth side

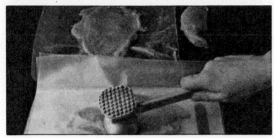

3 down, on sheet of waxed paper; cover with second sheet. Using a mallet or side of saucer, pound chicken to about ¼-inch thickness, being careful not to break the meat.

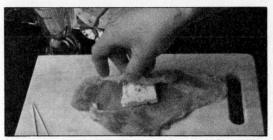

4 Cut frozen butter into 12 pats. Place a pat of herb butter in center of each piece of chicken. Bring long sides of chicken over butter; fold ends over, making sure that

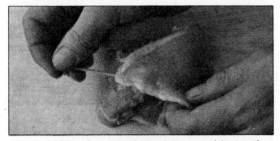

5 no butter is showing; fasten with toothpick. This is important to keep the herb butter inside during frying. Roll each chicken piece in the flour on a sheet of waxed paper.

6 Dip each in beaten egg; roll in crumbs, coating evenly. Then shape each piece, with palms of hands, into triangles (see Picture 7, below). Refrigerate, covered, until chilled—

7 about 1 hour. In a Dutch oven or large, heavy saucepan, slowly heat salad oil (3 inches deep) to 360F on deep-frying thermometer. Add chicken pieces, 3 at a time.

8 Fry, turning with tongs, till browned—5 minutes. Drain. (Do not pierce coating.) Keep warm in 200F oven 15 minutes (no more) in large pan lined with paper towels. Serves 8.

CHICKEN KIEV

HERB BUTTER
1 cup butter or regular margarine, softened
2 tablespoons chopped parsley
1½ teaspoons dried tarragon leaves

1 clove garlic, crushed
¾ teaspoon salt
⅛ teaspoon pepper
———————
6 boned whole chicken breasts (each ¾ lb)

¾ cup unsifted all-purpose flour
3 eggs, well beaten
1½ cups packaged dry bread crumbs
Salad oil or shortening for deep-frying

Arroz con pollo, that classic Spanish casserole of chicken, vegetables and saffron rice, has become a favorite dish throughout the world. We love it for its zesty flavor and the way it lends itself to easy, informal entertaining. It's colorful, economical and can be cooked and served in the same pot. And once it's in the oven, it requires very little attention—leaving you plenty of time to enjoy the party. Step-by-step instructions on the next page.

CHICKEN WITH A SPANISH ACCENT

1 Wash chicken pieces under cold running water; drain well. Wipe dry with paper towels so fat won't spatter when chicken is browning. Combine oregano, pepper and 2 teaspoons salt. Sprinkle chicken all over with mixture; rub in well. Let stand 10 minutes.

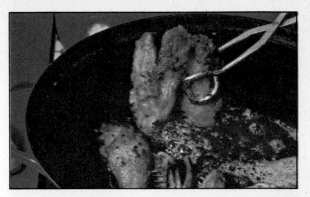

2 In heavy, 6-quart round or oval Dutch oven, heat olive oil over medium heat. Brown chicken, a third at a time, until golden-brown all over, using tongs to turn chicken—this takes about 30 minutes in all. Remove chicken as it browns. Preheat oven to 350F.

3 Wash green pepper; cut into quarters; remove ribs and seeds; cut into lengthwise strips, ¼ inch wide. To drippings in Dutch oven, add onion, garlic, green pepper, bay leaf and red pepper; sauté, stirring, over medium heat until onion is tender—5 minutes.

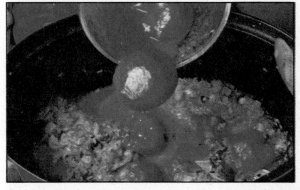

4 Using back of spoon, crush saffron threads on small piece of foil, or use a mortar and pestle. Add with 2 teaspoons salt and the rice to Dutch oven; cook, stirring, until rice is lightly browned—about 10 minutes. Add undrained tomatoes and chicken broth.

5 Arrange browned chicken pieces over rice mixture. Bring just to boiling, uncovered. Bake in oven, tightly covered, 1 hour. Remove from oven; add ½ cup water. Do not stir. Sprinkle peas and olives over top. Drain pimientos; cut into ¼-inch strips.

6 Arrange pimiento strips attractively over top. Bake, covered, 20 minutes longer, or until chicken is tender, peas are cooked and rice has absorbed all liquid. Remove from oven. Let stand, covered, 10 minutes. Serve right from Dutch oven. Serves 6.

ARROZ CON POLLO

2 (2½-lb size) roasting chickens, each cut into 6 pieces
2 teaspoons dried oregano leaves
½ teaspoon pepper
Salt
½ cup olive or salad oil
1 medium green pepper

2 cups chopped onion
1 clove garlic, crushed
1 bay leaf
⅛ to ¼ teaspoon crushed red pepper
1 teaspoon saffron threads
2 cups converted raw white rice

1 can (1 lb, 12 oz) tomatoes, undrained
1 can (13¾ oz) chicken broth
½ pkg (10-oz size) frozen green peas
½ cup pimiento-stuffed green olives, sliced
1 can (4 oz) pimientos

CURRYING FLAVOR

As a company dish, chicken curry has everything going for it. This is no ordinary curry, but a special blend that includes lime juice and grated lime peel, ginger, apple and cardamom to give a lift to prepared curry powder, and (chef's secret) there's a little chutney mixed into the sauce. It's relatively inexpensive to serve—chicken is still the most economical of meats—and can be made ahead and reheated. In fact, reheating improves the flavor. And the chicken breasts look spectacular served on a bed of saffron rice with slices of lime, surrounded by bowls of curry accompaniments for guests to choose from—coconut, pineapple, peanuts, slivered scallions, chutney and chopped green pepper.

1 Wash chicken; dry well on paper towels. Using a small sharp knife, carefully remove skin. Cut each breast in half, making 8. In ¼ cup hot butter in large skillet, over medium heat, brown chicken, 4 pieces at a time, 5 minutes per side. Using tongs,

2 remove chicken as it is browned. Return chicken to skillet. Add 1 can chicken broth; bring to boiling. Reduce heat; simmer, covered, 20 minutes, or just until tender. Remove chicken pieces; keep warm. Measure liquid in skillet; add remaining can of chicken

3 broth and water to make 3 cups; reserve. Make curry sauce: In ¼ cup hot butter in same skillet, sauté garlic, onion, curry powder, and apple until onion is tender—about 5 minutes. Remove from heat. Stir in flour, cardamom, ginger, salt, and pepper; mix

4 well. Gradually stir in reserved 3 cups liquid, lime peel and juice. Bring to boiling, stirring. Reduce heat; simmer, covered, 20 minutes, stirring occasionally. Stir in chutney; add chicken. Cover, and heat gently just to boiling, to reheat chicken—about 5 minutes.

5 Meanwhile, make saffron rice: Mix saffron with 2 tablespoons hot water; set aside. In hot oil and butter in medium saucepan, cook rice and salt, stirring occasionally, 5 minutes. Stir in the saffron mixture and 3 cups water; bring to boiling. Reduce

6 heat; simmer, covered, 15 to 20 minutes, or until liquid is absorbed. Turn rice into center of round platter. Arrange chicken breasts over rice; spoon sauce over chicken. Garnish with slices of lime. Serve with curry accompaniments. Makes 8 servings.

CHICKEN CURRY

4 whole chicken breasts (3¼ lb)
¼ cup butter or margarine
2 cans (10½-oz size) condensed chicken broth, undiluted

CURRY SAUCE
¼ cup butter or margarine
1 clove garlic, crushed
1 cup chopped onion

2 to 3 teaspoons curry powder
1 cup chopped pared tart apple
¼ cup unsifted all-purpose flour
¼ teaspoon ground cardamom
1 teaspoon ginger
½ teaspoon salt
¼ teaspoon pepper
2 teaspoons grated lime peel
2 tablespoons lime juice

¼ cup chopped chutney

SAFFRON RICE
¼ teaspoon saffron, crumbled
2 tablespoons olive or salad oil
2 tablespoons butter or margarine
1½ cups raw long-grain white rice
1½ teaspoons salt

A PERFECT
ONE-POT MEAL

Nothing warms a house like the aroma of a fragrant pot of chicken fricassee. Our creamy version, bursting with carrots and fluffy herbed dumplings, is a meal in itself. And it's not an expensive meal, either. We advise patting the chicken dry with paper towels to make it easier to brown. For really light dumplings, be sure to drop the batter on chicken pieces or vegetables—*not* in the liquid, where they'll get soggy. Step-by-step directions, next page.

GEORGE RATKAI

1 Wash chicken; dry on paper towels. If legs and thighs are large, cut apart. On waxed paper, combine flour with salt and marjoram; mix well. Dredge chicken in flour mixture, coating evenly. Shake off excess. Reserve leftover flour (about 2 tablespoons).

2 In 2 tablespoons hot butter in 6-quart Dutch oven, sauté chicken, four pieces at a time, skin side down, turning with tongs, until lightly browned all over—about 15 minutes. Lift out with tongs. Continue browning the chicken, adding butter as needed.

3 To drippings, add onion, celery, carrots, bay leaf, cloves and black peppers; sauté, stirring, 5 minutes. Stir in broth and 1 cup water; bring to boiling. Return chicken to Dutch oven. Bring to boiling; reduce heat; simmer, covered, 40 minutes.

4 Dumplings: In medium bowl, combine biscuit mix and 2 tablespoons chives; with fork, blend in egg and milk. Drop batter by 6 rounded tablespoonfuls, 2 to 3 inches apart, onto chicken (not in liquid). Cook, uncovered, over low heat 10 minutes.

5 Cover tightly; cook 10 minutes, or until dumplings are light and fluffy. With slotted spoon, lift dumplings to heated baking dish; keep warm in low oven. In small bowl, combine reserved flour mixture (see Step 1) with the light cream, stirring until smooth.

6 Stir flour mixture gently into fricassee; simmer 5 minutes, or until mixture is thickened. Replace dumplings on top of fricassee to serve. Reheat gently, covered, until hot. Before serving, sprinkle with more chives or parsley. Makes 6 servings.

CHICKEN FRICASSEE WITH DUMPLINGS

3 lb chicken parts (legs, thighs, breasts, wings)	**1 cup chopped celery**	**DUMPLINGS (6 large)**
⅓ cup flour	**6 large carrots, pared and halved**	**1½ cups packaged biscuit mix**
1½ teaspoons salt	**1 bay leaf**	**Snipped chives or chopped parsley**
1 teaspoon dried marjoram leaves	**4 whole cloves**	**1 egg**
¼ cup butter or margarine	**9 whole black peppers**	**¼ cup milk**
2 medium onions, sliced	**1 can (13¾ oz) chicken broth**	**½ cup light cream**

A TASTY WAY
TO TREAT A TURKEY

Turkey Tetrazzini was originally created for the Italian soprano Luisa Tetrazzini, back in the days when divas didn't count calories. Actually, the first version was made with chicken, but turkey gives it an even richer flavor. And what better way to use the remnants of a holiday bird? Pieces of cooked turkey are bathed in a rich wine-and-cream sauce, placed in a baking dish in a ring of spaghetti, topped with grated cheese and baked till hot. Or make it ahead of time, freeze and bake at the last minute.

44

1 Make sauce: Melt butter in large saucepan. Remove from heat. Stir in flour, 3 teaspoons salt and the nutmeg until smooth. Gradually add milk and turkey stock; bring to boiling, stirring constantly; boil 2 minutes, or until slightly thickened.

2 In small bowl, with wire whisk or wooden spoon, beat egg yolks with cream. Beat in a little of the hot mixture. Pour back into saucepan; cook over low heat, stirring constantly, until sauce is hot—do not boil. Remove from heat. Stir in the sherry.

3 Meanwhile, in 8-quart kettle, bring 6 quarts water to boiling; add 2 tablespoons salt and the spaghetti; cook as label directs; drain in colander. Return spaghetti to kettle. Add 2 cups sauce; toss lightly until spaghetti and sauce are well combined.

4 Divide spaghetti in half and place in two 12-by-8-by-2-inch baking dishes, arranging around edges. Add 2 cups sauce to turkey and mushrooms; mix well. Spoon half of turkey mixture into center of each dish. Reserve rest of sauce for later use.

5 Sprinkle cheese over spaghetti in each dish. Cover with foil; refrigerate 1 hour or overnight. About 1 hour before serving, preheat oven to 350F. Bake, covered, 45 minutes. Reheat sauce; spoon over spaghetti in each dish. Serves 12.

6 To freeze: Line baking dish with foil; assemble as directed. Fold foil over to seal; freeze right in dish. When frozen, lift out foil; remove dish from freezer. To serve: Unwrap; let stand 1 hour to thaw. Bake, covered, for 1 hour at 350F, or until bubbly.

TURKEY TETRAZZINI

SAUCE
¾ cup butter or margarine
¾ cup all-purpose flour
Salt
⅛ teaspoon nutmeg
1 quart milk
2 cups turkey stock* or

canned condensed chicken broth, undiluted
4 egg yolks
1 cup heavy cream
½ cup dry sherry

1 pkg (1 lb) thin spaghetti

6 cups cooked leftover turkey or chicken, cut into 1½-inch pieces
2 cans (6-oz size) whole mushrooms, drained
1 pkg (8oz) sharp Cheddar cheese, grated (2 cups)

*Turkey stock: Break up carcass. Place in 6-quart kettle with 3 cups water; 3 parsley sprigs; 2 carrots, pared and halved; 3 celery tops; 2 onions, halved; 2 teaspoons salt; 10 black peppercorns; 1 bay leaf. Bring to boiling; reduce heat; simmer, covered, 2 hours. Strain. Boil gently, uncovered, to reduce stock to 2 cups.

Cassoulet, a rich mélange of white beans, vegetables and various kinds of meat, is one of the greatest of French casseroles. It's traditionally made with goose, but there are infinite variations. We simmer the beans and vegetables with chicken, bacon and sausage in chicken broth and herbs. It's best prepared a day in advance and reheated. Serve with salad, bread and a fruit dessert. Step-by-step directions, next page.

A FABULOUS FRENCH CASSEROLE

46

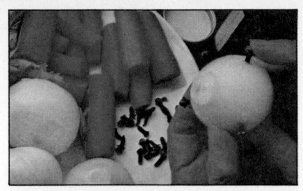

1 In an 8-quart kettle with cover, combine beans with 4½ cups cold water; let soak 2 hours, no longer. (They will burst easily in cooking.) Do not drain beans. Meanwhile, pare carrots; cut into quarters. Peel onions; stud 1 of the onions with whole cloves.

2 To beans, add chicken broth, bay leaves, ¼ of the carrots, the onions, onion studded with cloves, celery leaves, 1 teaspoon salt, the black peppers, garlic, thyme, marjoram and sage. Bring just to boiling; reduce heat and simmer, covered, 1 hour.

3 Add remaining carrots; cook, covered, 15 minutes longer. Meanwhile, cut bacon into two pieces. In large skillet, sauté bacon until browned, turning on all sides. Drain off fat. Preheat oven to 350F. Turn bean mixture into a 6-quart casserole. Add bacon.

4 Bake, uncovered, 30 minutes. Meanwhile, in hot butter in large skillet, brown chicken (half at a time), turning with tongs to brown well on all sides—this should take about 30 minutes in all. Sprinkle evenly with ½ teaspoon salt and ⅛ teaspoon pepper.

5 Add browned chicken and undrained tomatoes to beans. With sharp knife, cut 9 diagonal slashes, ⅛ inch deep, in top of sausage. Place sausage on top of chicken and vegetables. Cover tightly (you may use foil); bake 45 minutes, or until chicken is tender.

6 Bake, uncovered, 10 minutes longer. To serve, sprinkle with parsley. *Note:* Cassoulet is better made day before and refrigerated. To serve: Let warm to room temperature; reheat, covered, at 300F, 1 hour. (If too dry, add 1 cup chicken broth.) Serves 8.

CASSOULET

1½ lb Great Northern white beans	½ cup coarsely chopped celery leaves	½-lb bacon, unsliced
5 carrots	1½ teaspoons salt	4-lb roasting chicken, cut in 8 pieces
6 medium onions	3 whole black peppers	2 tablespoons butter or margarine
4 whole cloves	3 cloves garlic, crushed	⅛ teaspoon pepper
2 cans (10½-oz size) condensed	1½ teaspoons dried thyme leaves	1 can (1 lb) peeled tomatoes, undrained
chicken broth, undiluted	1 teaspoon dried marjoram leaves	1 lb Polish sausage (whole)
2 bay leaves, crumbled	1 teaspoon dried sage leaves	2 tablespoons chopped parsley

For an Easter dinner that's an exciting change, try this classic duckling à l'orange. Our version of the famous French dish is stuffed with orange, onion—and just a hint of garlic. To make it all the more flavorful, it's served with a brandy-laced orange sauce. We carve it a special way, removing the wishbone and slicing diagonally, so that one duckling will feed four people generously.

DELICIOUS DUCK À L'ORANGE

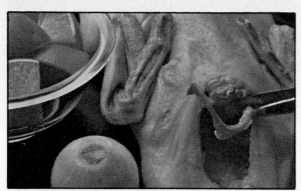

1 Remove giblets and neck from duckling and reserve. Wash duckling under running water; drain; dry with paper towels. Turn breast side down; using sharp scissors and knife, carefully cut out wishbone from breast for easier carving. Preheat oven to 425F.

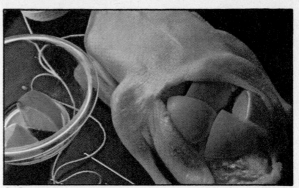

2 Sprinkle inside with ½ teaspoon salt. Tuck onion inside neck; bring skin of neck over back. Fasten with poultry pins. Stuff body cavity with garlic, black peppers and oranges. Close cavity with poultry pins. Tie legs together; bend wing tips under body.

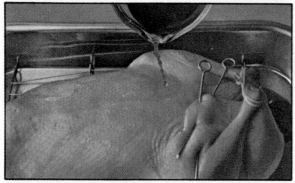

3 Place on rack in shallow roasting pan. Pour ½ cup Burgundy over duckling. Roast, uncovered, 30 minutes. Reduce oven to 375F; roast 1½ hours. Bring giblets to boiling in 2 cups water and ½ teaspoon salt; reduce heat; simmer, covered, 1 hour. Strain.

4 Sauce: In 2 tablespoons butter in skillet, brown liver. Remove from heat. Heat brandy slightly. Ignite; pour over liver. Remove liver; chop. In same skillet, in rest of butter, sauté orange peel and garlic 3 minutes. Stir in flour, catsup, bouillon cube and pepper.

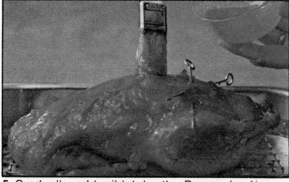

5 Gradually add giblet broth, Burgundy, ¼ cup marmalade and the orange juice; mix well. Bring to boiling; reduce heat; simmer, stirring, 15 minutes. Add liver and orange sections; heat. Spread duckling with ½ cup marmalade; roast 10 minutes longer.

6 Remove pins and twine. Place on heated platter. Using sharp knife, cut each side of breast into diagonal slices, ½ inch wide, starting at leg. Then run knife down center of breast to separate two sides; run knife around outer edge to cut skin. Pass sauce.

DUCKLING À L'ORANGE

5-lb ready-to-cook duckling (if frozen, thaw completely)	**ORANGE SAUCE**	1 chicken-bouillon cube
1 teaspoon salt	3 tablespoons butter or margarine	Dash pepper
1 large onion, peeled	Liver from duckling	1¼ cups broth from giblets
1 clove garlic, chopped	3 tablespoons brandy	⅓ cup Burgundy
3 whole black peppers	2 tablespoons grated orange peel	¼ cup orange marmalade
2 unpeeled oranges, quartered	¾ teaspoon chopped garlic	¼ cup orange juice
½ cup Burgundy	2 tablespoons flour	1 cup orange sections
	2 teaspoons catsup	½ cup orange marmalade

Note: If desired, roast 2 ducklings at same time, leaving sauce recipe as is. Nice served with white rice combined with sautéed sliced mushrooms.

SOME LIKE IT HOT

It may be the middle of summer, but you can't always satisfy a hungry family with sandwiches and cold soup. Outdoor activities build up big appetites, and this often calls for hot, filling meals, tasty but not too expensive. Here are three new ideas: Rib pork chops filled with a fragrant herb-and-raisin stuffing; cabbage leaves rolled around an unusual beef-veal-rice combination and flavored with onions, mushrooms and a touch of garlic; and, for lovers of Italian food, tangy chicken cacciatore. We serve ours with polenta—cooked yellow cornmeal.

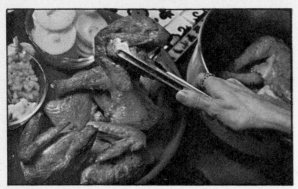

1 Wash chicken; pat dry with paper towels. Heat oil and butter in 5- or 6-quart Dutch oven. Add chicken to hot fat, a few pieces at a time; brown well, turning on all sides. With tongs, remove pieces as they are browned and set aside—takes about 10 minutes in all.

2 Add onion, garlic, carrot, celery, parsley, salt, pepper, bay leaf and basil to Dutch oven. Sauté, stirring, until golden-brown—about 5 minutes. Add tomatoes and tomato sauce; mix well, mashing tomatoes with a fork. Bring to boiling, stirring.

3 Reduce heat; simmer, uncovered, 20 minutes. Add browned chicken with drippings and wine; gently simmer, covered, 45 to 50 minutes, until tender. Make polenta: In heavy, 6-quart kettle, bring 4 cups water and the salt to a full, rolling boil.

4 Slowly add cornmeal to the boiling water (it should not stop boiling), stirring constantly with wire whisk—mixture will become very thick. Turn heat very low; cook, uncovered and without stirring, until a very thick crust forms and leaves side of the pan.

5 This takes about 20 minutes. Spoon into a lightly greased, 9-inch, 1½-quart casserole, spreading evenly. (Keep warm in low oven if not serving at once.) To serve: With spatula, loosen around edge and underneath. Invert on large, heated platter.

6 Shake gently to release polenta in a large mound. Spoon chicken and some of sauce around polenta. Pass rest of sauce in gravy boat. If desired, sprinkle with chopped parsley. For each person, serve a chicken quarter with polenta and sauce. Serves 8.

CHICKEN CACCIATORE WITH POLENTA

2 (2-lb size) ready-to-cook broiler-fryers, quartered	½ cup pared, chopped carrot	1 can (1 lb, 1 oz) Italian tomatoes, undrained
3 tablespoons olive or salad oil	½ cup chopped celery	1 can (8 oz) tomato sauce
2 tablespoons butter or margarine	2 tablespoons chopped parsley	½ cup red wine
1½ cups sliced onion	1½ teaspoons salt	**POLENTA**
1 clove garlic, crushed	¼ teaspoon pepper	1 tablespoon salt
	1 bay leaf	2 cups yellow cornmeal
	½ teaspoon dried basil	

1 Make stuffing: Trim some of crust from bread; cut bread into ¼-inch cubes. In ¼ cup hot butter in large skillet, sauté the chopped onion and celery, stirring, until onion is golden—about 5 minutes. Add bread cubes; stir to combine. Remove skillet from heat.

2 Add parsley, raisins, 1½ teaspoons salt, the marjoram and pepper; toss lightly to combine. Preheat oven to 350F. Wipe pork chops with damp paper towels. Trim excess fat; reserve. Using sharp paring knife, cut a pocket in each chop, all the way to rib.

3 Fill each pocket with ¼ cup stuffing; fasten together with two wooden picks. On a sheet of waxed paper, mix together the flour and 1 teaspoon salt. Coat the pork chops on both sides with flour mixture; reserve rest of flour mixture to use in making gravy.

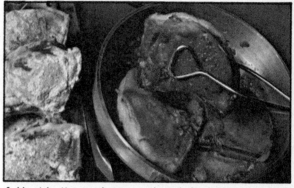

4 Heat butter and reserved pork fat in large skillet. Over low heat, brown chops well on both sides, turning with tongs—about 10 minutes on each side. Cook three at one time. Remove; brown rest of chops. Pour off fat. Add wine, juice or cider to skillet.

5 Stir over medium heat to dissolve browned bits. Pour into bottom of 13-by-9-by-2-inch roasting pan. Stand chops in bottom of pan. Cover with foil. Bake 1 hour. Remove from oven; discard wooden picks. Bake chops, uncovered, 40 minutes, or until tender.

6 Remove chops to platter; keep warm. Make gravy: Over medium heat, boil drippings, uncovered, 10 minutes, to reduce to 1 cup. Dissolve reserved flour mixture in ½ cup water. Add to drippings; bring to boiling, stirring; simmer 3 minutes. Strain. Serves 6.

BAKED STUFFED PORK CHOPS

STUFFING

4 slices day-old bread
¼ cup butter or margarine
½ cup finely chopped onion
½ cup finely chopped celery

2 tablespoons chopped parsley
½ cup dark raisins
1½ teaspoons salt
1 teaspoon dried marjoram
 leaves
⅛ teaspoon pepper

6 rib pork chops, 1½ inches
thick (each about ¾ lb)
¼ cup all-purpose flour, salt
2 tablespoons butter
1 cup white wine, apple juice
or cider

1 In 8-quart kettle, bring 6 cups water to boiling. Meanwhile, carefully remove 12 outer leaves from cabbage. Add leaves and 1 teaspoon salt to boiling water; simmer 3 minutes—long enough to make leaves pliable. Drain leaves, reserving 2 cups liquid.

2 If leaves are not pliable or soft enough to roll, return to boiling water for a minute or two. Trim thick rib. Make stuffing: Melt ¼ cup butter in a large, heavy skillet. Add the chopped onion; sauté, stirring with a large wooden spoon, until it is golden—3 minutes.

3 Add ¼ cup butter, along with the garlic and mushrooms; sauté, stirring occasionally, about 4 minutes. Add chuck, veal, rice, eggs, 1 teaspoon salt and dash pepper; cook, uncovered and stirring, about 5 minutes, or until meat is no longer red.

4 Make tomato sauce: Melt butter in medium saucepan; remove from heat. Stir in flour until smooth; gradually stir in tomato paste combined with the 2 cups reserved cabbage liquid. Over medium heat, bring to boiling, stirring with wooden spoon.

5 Stir in salt, pepper and allspice; remove from heat. Preheat oven to 350F. Place ½ cup of the meat mixture in the hollow of each of the 12 cabbage leaves. Fold the sides of leaf over the stuffing; roll up from the thick end of the leaf to make a neat roll.

6 Arrange cabbage rolls, seam side down, in a single layer in lightly greased, shallow, 3-quart casserole. Pour sauce over all. Bake, covered, 50 minutes; uncovered, 10 minutes. Remove to warm serving platter; spoon sauce over all. Serves 8.

STUFFED CABBAGE ROLLS

1 large head green cabbage (3 lb)
1 teaspoon salt

STUFFING
½ cup butter or margarine
1 cup chopped onion
1 clove garlic, crushed

½ lb fresh mushrooms, sliced
½ lb ground chuck
½ lb ground veal
1½ cups cooked white rice
3 hard-cooked eggs, chopped
1 teaspoon salt
Dash pepper

TOMATO SAUCE
¼ cup butter or margarine
¼ cup unsifted all-purpose flour
1 can (6 oz) tomato paste
½ teaspoon salt
Dash pepper
¼ teaspoon allspice

THE SAUCES

Hollandaise and Béarnaise are the aristocrats of sauces. Hollandaise is a rich, tart mayonnaiselike sauce, an emulsion of egg yolks, butter, and lemon juice. It's wonderful with asparagus, broccoli, artichokes, and green beans, as well as with fish, cold veal, and chicken. Its near relative, Béarnaise, is also made with egg yolks and butter, but flavored with tarragon and white wine. Serve Béarnaise with broiled steak or lamb chops, or use it to turn hamburgers into something elegant. Both sauces have a reputation for being very difficult to make, but they're not—if you carefully follow our step-by-step directions.

1 In top of double boiler, with wire whisk, beat egg yolks with 2 tablespoons cold water just until blended. Cook over hot, not boiling, water, stirring constantly with whisk, until mixture begins to thicken—about 1 minute. Add butter, 1 tablespoon at

2 a time (cut stick of butter into 8 pieces), beating continuously after each addition until butter is melted and mixture is smooth before adding next piece of butter—takes about 5 minutes in all. Hot water in double-boiler base should not touch

3 bottom of pan above; water should not be allowed to boil. (If it should start to bubble, add a little cold water at once to cool it.) Sauce curdles easily over high heat. Remove double-boiler top from hot water before adding lemon. Using a

4 wire whisk, slowly beat in lemon juice, then salt and cayenne, beating just until sauce becomes thick as mayonnaise. To keep warm: Add cold water to hot water in bottom of double boiler to make luke-warm; replace sauce, covered, over water, not heat.

5 To make Béarnaise: In small saucepan, combine vinegar, wine, tarragon, shallots, pepper, and parsley; bring to boiling, stirring. Reduce heat, and simmer, uncovered, to reduce to ¼ cup—about 8 minutes. Strain into a measuring cup, pressing

6 herbs to extract juice. Let cool. Cook egg yolks, as in Step 1, using 2 tablespoons tarragon liquid for water. Continue with Steps 2, 3, and 4, using 2 tablespoons tarragon liquid for lemon. Add chopped herb. Serve warm or cold. Makes 1 cup.

THE DIFFICULT SAUCES

HOLLANDAISE SAUCE
3 egg yolks
2 tablespoons cold water
½ cup (1 stick) butter or
regular margarine
2   tablespoons lemon juice
⅛ teaspoon salt
Dash cayenne

BÉARNAISE SAUCE
¼ cup tarragon vinegar
¼ cup dry white wine
2 tablespoons finely chopped
fresh tarragon or 2 teaspoons
dried tarragon leaves
1 tablespoon chopped
shallot or onion

⅛ teaspoon coarsely ground
black pepper
1 tablespoon chopped parsley
3 egg yolks
½ cup (1 stick) butter or
regular margarine
1 tablespoon chopped
fresh tarragon or parsley

1 In heavy, medium-size saucepan, slowly heat butter just until melted, not browned, stirring with wooden spoon. (For a savory sauce, add 1 tablespoon chopped onion to butter; cook, stirring, until golden and tender, not browned—about 5 minutes.) Remove

2 from heat. Gradually add flour, salt and pepper; stir until smooth. (Combining fat and flour first prevents lumping.) Add milk, stirring to mix well. (Liquid may be light cream, chicken broth, fish stock or wine, depending on sauce. Add cold liquids all at

3 once. Add hot liquids gradually, stirring after each addition.) Return to heat. Over medium heat, bring to boiling, stirring constantly, until thickened; reduce heat; simmer 3 minutes, stirring. (Sauce must come to boiling and be held there briefly to cook flour so

4 it thickens sauce and does not have a raw taste.) Makes 2 cups. Cheese Sauce: Add ½ teaspoon dry mustard, 2 cups grated sharp Cheddar cheese and dash cayenne to white sauce. Stir over low heat until cheese melts and sauce is smooth. Nice over

5 broccoli, cauliflower, asparagus and egg dishes. Deluxe Cream Sauce: In medium bowl, beat 2 egg yolks. Stir in about ½ cup of the hot white sauce; mix well. Return egg-yolk mixture to rest of sauce in saucepan, stirring constantly. Cook, stirring, over low heat

6 until thickened; do not boil. To keep sauce hot, cover and place over hot water. Horseradish Sauce: Add ⅓ cup undrained prepared horseradish, 1 tablespoon lemon juice and dash cayenne to basic sauce. Heat, stirring to combine. Nice with beef, ham or tongue.

PERFECT SAUCES

¼ **cup butter or regular margarine**	2 **cups milk or light cream**	**DELUXE CREAM SAUCE**
¼ **cup unsifted all-purpose flour**	**CHEESE SAUCE**	2 **egg yolks**
	½ **teaspoon dry mustard**	**HORSERADISH SAUCE**
½ **teaspoon salt**	2 **cups grated natural sharp Cheddar cheese (½ lb)**	⅓ **cup prepared horseradish**
⅛ **teaspoon pepper**	**Dash cayenne**	1 **tablespoon lemon juice**
		Dash cayenne

Note: Stir constantly for a sauce that is very smooth; this will also prevent it from becoming too thick. Taste before serving to correct seasoning. For a richer flavor, stir in a tablespoon of butter just at the end.

ELEGANT BRAISED BEEF:

A SURPRISE IN EVERY SLICE

GEORGE RATKAI

Larding—running strips of marinated salt pork or bacon through a lean roast for extra tenderness and flavor—is an old chef's secret well worth reviving. It's coe surprise in this very elegant beef a la mode, which is larded not only with pork but with carrot strips as well, so that when it's carved, there's a round of carrot embedded in each slice. Some general tips: brown meat slowly on all sides—in a heavy utensil, with enough fat to cover the bottom of the pan. Use a Dutch oven just large enough for the roast—liquid should only come halfway up the side of the roast; otherwise meat will be boiled, not braised. Serve roast with pan liquid. Skim the fat first, then reduce it to one half of original volume by boiling rapidly, uncovered.

1 Cut salt pork and carrots into strips 3 inches long and ¼ inch thick. In small bowl, mix·chopped onion, garlic, parsley, bay leaf, 2 teaspoons salt, and 1 teaspoon pepper.

2 Toss salt pork, several strips at a time, in onion mixture. Make marinade: In 1-quart measure, combine red wine, whole bay leaf, salt, pepper, and thyme; stir to mix well.

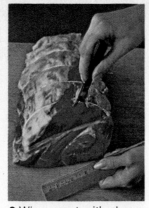

3 Wipe roast with damp paper towels. Then, with a sharp, pointed knife, make slits in surface of the roast, at 2-inch intervals, 3½ to 4 inches deep and ½ inch wide.

4 Push a pork strip into each slit. Insert a carrot strip in front of each; carrots should face narrow end, to show when roast is sliced. Reserve any leftover onion mixture.

5 Place roast in large plastic food container. Add marinade and leftover onion mixture. Refrigerate, covered, 6 hours, or overnight, turning meat several times.

6 Preheat oven to 350F. Remove roast; wipe dry; reserve marinade. In hot oil in 5- or 6-quart Dutch oven, brown roast on all sides, turning with wooden spoons—takes a half

7 hour. Pour reserved marinade and beef broth over meat. Add onion stuck with cloves. Liquid should reach about halfway up side of roast. Insert a meat thermometer

8 into the thickest part. Roast, covered, 1 hour. Uncover; roast, basting occasionally, about 2½ hours, or until fork-tender. Meat is medium-rare at 150F on thermometer.

9 One and a half hours before meat is done, add carrots and onions to hot butter and sugar in large skillet. Stir over medium heat 10 minutes. Add to roast; cook until tender.

BEEF A LA MODE

¼ lb salt pork
2 medium carrots, pared
½ cup finely chopped onion
1 clove garlic, crushed
2 tablespoons chopped parsley
1 bay leaf, crushed
2 teaspoons salt
1 teaspoon pepper
2 cups dry red wine
1 bay leaf
1 teaspoon salt
¼ teaspoon pepper
½ teaspoon dried thyme
leaves
6-lb top or bottom round beef
pot roast
¼ cup salad or olive oil
1 can (10½ oz) condensed
beef broth, undiluted
1 peeled medium onion, stuck
with 6 whole cloves
8 medium carrots, pared and
halved crosswise
16 small white onions, peeled
2 tablespoons butter
2 tablespoons sugar

PERFECT POT ROAST

1 Wipe pot roast with damp paper towels. In hot oil and butter in 5-quart Dutch oven or heavy kettle, over medium heat, brown roast along with sliced onion (onion browns and gives a good dark color and rich flavor to pan drippings), turning roast with

2 two wooden spoons, until well browned on all sides —25 minutes in all. Slow browning gives the meat and gravy a better flavor and color. To drippings in Dutch oven, add garlic, thyme, marjoram, bay leaf, black peppers and salt; stir ½ minute (this

3 restores flavor to herbs, and meat absorbs seasonings). Add beef broth (you may substitute tomato juice, stewed tomatoes, beer or red wine to vary the flavor). Bring to boiling; then reduce heat to simmer (cook just below the boiling point), covered,

4 for 2½ hours. Turn meat occasionally so that it will cook evenly. Add carrots, onions and parsley; simmer, covered, 30 minutes, or until vegetables and meat are tender. To make gravy: Remove meat and vegetables from Dutch oven to a warm platter; keep in

5 a warm place, covered loosely with foil. Pour ¼ cup water into measuring cup; add flour; mix with fork until smooth. (If flour is added to the water, it will dissolve more easily.) Strain liquid remaining in Dutch oven. If necessary, add water to measure 2

6 cups. Return to Dutch oven. Stir flour mixture into liquid in Dutch oven; bring to boiling, stirring. Reduce heat; simmer 3 minutes. Taste; add salt, if desired. Spoon a little of the gravy over meat; then pass with vegetables. Nice with boiled potatoes. Serves 10.

PERFECT POT ROAST

4-to-5-lb beef rump roast	1 teaspoon dried thyme leaves	1 can (10½ oz) condensed
2 tablespoons salad oil	1 teaspoon dried marjoram	beef broth, undiluted (1⅓ cups)
2 tablespoons butter or	leaves	8 halved, pared carrots (1 lb)
regular margarine	1 bay leaf, crumbled	12 small white onions, peeled
1 small onion, sliced	8 whole black peppers	1 sprig parsley
1 clove garlic, crushed	1 teaspoon salt	3 tablespoons flour

Braising is a method of cooking the less tender cuts of beef—it is first browned in a small amount of fat, and then it is simmered for several hours in a small amount of liquid until it is deliciously tender.

THE SHAKER WAY WITH STEW

The Shakers cultivated herbs extensively. They grew medicinal herbs for their own remedies, and were also the largest suppliers of these herbs to the pharmaceutical companies of the time. They grew and marketed kitchen herbs, too, harvesting them by the acre and selling them in the United States and abroad. "Why send to Europe's distant shores/for plants which grow at our own doors?" asked a persuasive couplet in an 1883 catalogue of Shaker goods. By their inventive use of herbs in an era of plain cooking, they anticipated the twentieth-century American gourmet by a good hundred years. The beef stew pictured here is a delicious example of the Shaker way with flavorings. The light-as-air dumplings are flecked with parsley (or marjoram, chives, or chervil). The stew itself takes its hearty flavor as well as its substance from carrots, celery, and onions. The recipe and step-by-step pictured instructions for making it are on the following page.

1 On waxed paper, roll beef cubes in flour mixed with salt and pepper, coating evenly on all sides. Reserve remaining flour mixture for later. In hot butter in 6-quart Dutch oven, brown beef well on all sides, turning with tongs. Do not overcrowd. As

2 beef is browned, remove, and set aside. Continue browning rest. Takes 30 minutes in all to give good rich flavor and brown color. Return beef to Dutch oven; add bay leaf, thyme, chopped celery, onion with cloves, parsley sprigs. Toss to coat with drippings.

3 Add **5** cups water; bring to boiling; reduce heat, and simmer, covered, 2 hours. Add onions, carrots, and potatoes; simmer, covered, 20 minutes; add turnips and celery; simmer 10 minutes. During this 10 minutes, make dumplings: In medium bowl, combine

4 biscuit mix and parsley; stir in egg and milk, mixing with fork just until blended. Drop batter by 10 rounded tablespoonfuls onto gently boiling stew (on meat or vegetables, not in liquid—this makes dumplings soggy), 2 to 3 inches apart, allowing room

5 for expansion. Cook, uncovered, over low heat 10 minutes. Cover tightly; cook 10 minutes longer. Using slotted spoon, remove dumplings to heated baking dish; keep warm in oven while thickening the stew: In small bowl, combine 3 tablespoons reserved

6 flour mixture (see Step 1) with ¼ cup water, stirring until smooth. Stir gently into stew; simmer 5 minutes, or until the mixture is thickened. Replace dumplings on top of stew to serve. Reheat gently, covered, until thoroughly hot. Makes 8 to 10 servings.

BEEF STEW WITH PARSLEY DUMPLINGS

3 lb boneless chuck or round,
cut into 1- to 1½-inch cubes
⅓ cup all-purpose flour
2½ teaspoons salt
¼ teaspoon pepper
¼ cup butter or margarine
1 bay leaf
1½ teaspoons dried thyme
leaves
½ cup chopped celery tops

1 small onion, stuck with 4
whole cloves
2 parsley sprigs
1 lb peeled small yellow
onions (about 8)
1 lb medium carrots (about 5),
pared and halved crosswise
1½ lb small new potatoes,
pared or scrubbed
with skins on (about 10)

2 medium white turnips,
pared and quartered, or 4 small,
pared and halved
1½ cups celery, cut into
1-inch pieces
PARSLEY DUMPLINGS:
2 cups packaged biscuit mix
2 tablespoons chopped parsley
1 egg
½ cup milk

A CLASSIC FRENCH STEW

Thrifty French housewives have always used every scrap of an animal, right down to the tail. Oxtail, a long-neglected but delicious cut, is now appearing in supermarkets. Take advantage of the low price to make a rich, nutritious ragout. Oxtails must be braised long and lovingly to develop full flavor. But the dish tastes even better made ahead and reheated.

1 Day before: Wash oxtails under cold water; dry with paper towels. In some of hot butter in a 5-quart Dutch oven, brown oxtails, half at a time, turning with tongs to brown well all over; add butter as needed. Lift out the oxtails as they are browned.

2 (Slow browning gives better flavor and color—takes about 30 minutes in all.) To fat in Dutch oven, add chopped vegetables, garlic, peppers, salt, thyme and bay leaves. Sauté over medium heat, stirring, until onion is golden—about 5 minutes.

3 Add browned oxtails, beef broth and 2 cups water. Bring to boiling; reduce heat; simmer, covered, over low heat 3 hours, or until oxtails are tender. Remove from heat; stir in wine. Cool to room temperature; refrigerate, covered, overnight.

4 Next day, about an hour before serving: With metal spoon, skim off hardened layer of fat from surface and discard. Heat oxtails slowly over low heat, stirring occasionally; bring just to boiling point. Meanwhile, prepare carrots and potatoes.

5 Add carrots and potatoes; bring back to boiling; reduce heat and simmer, covered, until vegetables are tender when pierced with fork—30 minutes. Ten minutes before cooking time is up, cook frozen peas following directions on package label; drain.

6 To ¼ cup flour in small bowl, stir in ½ cup cold water; mix with fork until smooth. Stir into bubbling liquid in Dutch oven. Simmer, stirring occasionally, until sauce has thickened—about 5 minutes. Sprinkle top of the ragout with peas. Serves 8.

OXTAIL RAGOUT

4 lb oxtails, cut crosswise in 2-inch pieces (if frozen, let thaw)	¼ teaspoon whole black peppers	1 cup red Burgundy
¼ cup butter or margarine	2 teaspoons salt	8 to 10 small carrots (1½ lb), pared and cut into 1½-inch pieces
1 cup chopped carrot	1 teaspoon dried thyme leaves	12 new potatoes (1½ lb), washed, partially pared
1 cup chopped celery	2 bay leaves	1 pkg (10-oz size) frozen peas
1 cup chopped onion	2 cans (10½-oz size) condensed beef broth, undiluted	¼ cup all-purpose flour
1 clove garlic, crushed		

Osso buco, in Italian, means marrowbone, the round bone in the shin of a calf, and in Milan they have a way of preparing this modest cut of meat that has become world-famous. Veal shanks are braised in tomato sauce and wine, with herbs, vegetables and garlic, then garnished with a combination of parsley, celery, garlic and lemon peel that gives the dish its distinctive piquant flavor. Osso buco makes a hearty meal served with rice and a green salad. And there's a bonus: The marrow in the bones is delicious. Instructions, following page.

A HEARTY ITALIAN DISH

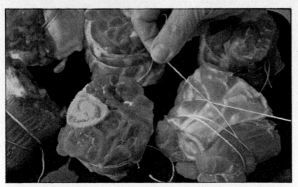

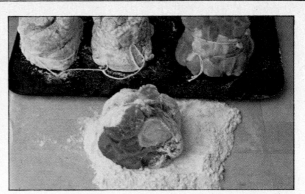

1 Have butcher cross-cut 2 veal shinbones full of marrow into 3-inch pieces, to make 6 servings. Wipe the veal shanks with damp paper towels. Tie each with string to hold meat together. On sheet of waxed paper, combine flour, salt, and pepper; rub

2 into veal shanks, coating them well on all sides. In hot butter and oil in 5-quart Dutch oven, over medium heat, brown veal shanks, 3 at a time, turning to brown well on all sides—30 minutes. Remove shanks as they are browned; set aside. To drippings

3 in Dutch oven, add onion, carrot, diced celery, and 2 cloves garlic; sauté, stirring, until onion is tender— 5 minutes. Add tomato sauce, wine, basil, thyme, parsley sprigs, and bay leaf. Bring mixture to boiling. Reduce heat; add browned veal shanks; using tongs,

4 place in upright position so that round bone with marrow faces up. The liquid should come halfway up the veal shanks. Simmer, covered, 2½ hours, or until veal is very tender. Meanwhile, prepare gremolata: In small bowl, combine parsley, celery, grated lemon

5 peel, and garlic. Mix well. Add half of the gremolata to cooked veal shanks; simmer, covered, 5 minutes. Remove strings. Place veal shanks on warm serving dish. Spoon some of sauce in bottom of pan over veal shanks; pass rest. Sprinkle with remaining gremolata.

6 Serve with hot rice or pasta tossed with butter and Parmesan cheese. Serve with a seafood-cocktail fork or marrow spoon for spooning out marrow. (Marrow may be spread on small chunks of bread.) Makes 6 servings. This is even better reheated the next day.

OSSO BUCO

6 (¾-to-1-lb size) veal shanks	1 cup coarsely chopped onion	3 parsley sprigs
¼ cup flour	1 cup thinly sliced, pared carrot	1 bay leaf
2 teaspoons salt	½ cup diced celery	
¼ teaspoon pepper	2 cloves garlic, crushed	**GREMOLATA**
3 tablespoons butter or regular margarine	1 can (8 oz) tomato sauce	2 tablespoons chopped parsley
3 tablespoons olive or salad oil	1 cup dry white wine	2 tablespoons chopped celery
	1 teaspoon dried basil leaves	1 tablespoon grated lemon peel
	1 teaspoon dried thyme leaves	1 teaspoon crushed garlic

Lamb Stew with Vegetables and Party Meat Loaf

A robust lamb stew with vegetables; a party meat loaf made from ground beef and pork with a surprise carrot filling and a rich tomato glaze (not to mention a new way to prepare green beans)

1 Wipe lamb with damp paper towels. On waxed paper, combine flour, salt and pepper; coat lamb evenly with flour mixture. Reserve leftover flour. In hot butter in 6-quart Dutch oven, brown lamb, a third at a time, well, along with quartered onion and garlic.

2 Turn lamb with tongs; lift out as it browns. Continue until all lamb is browned, adding more butter if needed (takes about ½ hour in all). Add onions, mushrooms and sugar to drippings in Dutch oven. Cook, covered, 5 minutes, or until lightly browned.

3 Return lamb to Dutch oven; add thyme, parsley and bay leaf. Toss with drippings to coat evenly. Stir in 2 cups water and 1 cup wine. Place a large sheet of waxed paper over top of Dutch oven. Place lid on top of paper, letting it hang over. Bring to boiling.

4 Reduce heat; simmer, covered, 40 minutes. (To keep from diluting sauce, pour off any liquid collecting on top of paper during cooking.) Meanwhile, pare carrots; cut each into three pieces. Scrub potatoes; pare a 1-inch band of skin from center of each potato.

5 Add carrots and potatoes to lamb; stir to combine. Bring back to boiling. Reduce heat; simmer, covered, 40 minutes, or until meat and all of the vegetables are tender when pierced with a fork. Remove from heat and skim any fat from the surface.

6 Combine reserved flour mixture and ½ cup red wine; stir into liquid in Dutch oven. Simmer, covered, 10 to 15 minutes, or until slightly thickened. Remove from heat. Add a little more wine to thin sauce, if necessary. Sprinkle with chopped parsley. Serves 8.

LAMB STEW WITH VEGETABLES

2½ lb boneless lamb, cut into 1½-inch pieces	1 clove garlic, crushed	2 sprigs parsley
⅓ cup all-purpose flour	12 medium yellow onions, peeled (1¼ lb)	1 large bay leaf
2½ teaspoons salt	8 medium whole mushrooms	1½ cups red wine
¼ teaspoon pepper	1 teaspoon sugar	1 lb carrots (5 or 6)
¼ cup butter or margarine	1¼ teaspoons dried thyme leaves	1¼ lb small new potatoes (about 8)
1 medium onion, quartered		Chopped parsley

1 In 1 inch boiling water in large saucepan, cook carrots, covered, 25 minutes, or until tender. Drain; mash; measure 3 cups. In hot butter in skillet, sauté chopped onion, stirring, until golden. Combine half of onion with carrot, 1 teaspoon salt, dash pepper.

2 Preheat oven to 350F. In large bowl, combine eggs, bread crumbs, milk, thyme, 1 tablespoon salt, ¼ teaspoon pepper; mix well. Add ground beef, pork, parsley and rest of onion; mix well. Roll out between two sheets of waxed paper placed on damp surface.

3 Roll to form a rectangle 14 by 10 inches, ¼ inch thick. Remove top sheet of waxed paper. Spread meat evenly with carrot filling; roll up as for jelly roll, starting with narrow edge. Place the meat loaf, seam side down, in shallow roasting pan lined with foil.

4 Make glaze: In small bowl, combine catsup, brown sugar and mustard; mix well. Brush over meat loaf. Bake, uncovered, 1 hour. Meanwhile, in 1 inch boiling water with ½ teaspoon salt in large skillet, cook whole onions, covered, about 25 minutes; drain.

5 Wash green beans; trim ends. Using string, tie beans into bundles, ten in each. In large skillet, in 1 inch boiling water and 1 teaspoon salt, boil beans gently, covered, 12 to 15 minutes, or until tender. Drain. Remove strings when on serving platter.

6 In skillet, melt 2 tablespoons butter with granulated sugar. Add onions; over medium heat, sauté, turning, until golden-brown—about 5 minutes. Arrange meat loaf and vegetables on warm platter. Pour ¼ cup melted butter over beans. Serves 8 to 10.

PARTY MEAT LOAF (See page 68 for illustration.)

2 lb carrots, pared and cut up	½ teaspoon dried thyme leaves	2 tablespoons brown sugar
¼ cup butter or margarine	1 tablespoon salt	¼ teaspoon dry mustard
1 cup finely chopped onion	¼ teaspoon pepper	
1 teaspoon salt, dash pepper	1½ lb ground beef	10 medium onions, peeled
	½ lb ground lean pork	Salt
2 eggs	2 tablespoons chopped parsley	1½ lb fresh green beans
1 cup grated day-old-bread crumbs		Butter or margarine
¼ cup milk	½ cup catsup	1 tablespoon granulated sugar

1 Day ahead: Wipe veal with damp paper towels. Trim off fat. Spread meat flat, skin side down; rub with salt and pepper. Sprinkle with thyme, lemon juice. Make fillings. Preheat oven to 325F. Spread spinach filling evenly over meat, 1 inch from edge.

2 Then spread the veal with a layer of ham filling. Starting at short side, roll up; tie with string at 1½-inch intervals. Place in shallow roasting pan, seam side down. Roast, uncovered, 1 hour. Remove from oven; pour white wine over the veal.

3 Cover pan tightly with foil. Bake 1½ hours, or until tender when tested with fork. Remove from oven.** Cool in pan. Remove; wrap in foil; refrigerate overnight. Next day, make glaze: In small saucepan, sprinkle gelatine over ¾ cup broth to soften.

4 Over low heat, stir broth to dissolve gelatine. Add remaining broth; pour 2 cups into a 9-by-9-by-2-inch pan. Add Madeira. Chill until firm—2 hours. Set rest of broth in saucepan into bowl of ice; add mayonnaise; beat with whisk until smooth.

5 Stir occasionally until thick as unbeaten egg white. Set veal on rack on tray; remove string. Spoon thickened glaze over. Set veal on rack on clean tray. Refrigerate to set—½ hour. Scrape glaze from tray; reheat; chill until slightly thick.

6 Use to give veal a second coat. Press carrot, green pepper and capers into glaze, as pictured. Place on chilled platter. Cut aspic into ½-inch cubes. Spoon around veal. Refrigerate until serving. Slice thinly; serve with aspic cubes. Serves 8.

BREAST OF VEAL CHAUDFROID (See page 86 for illustration and filling.)

3½-to-4-lb boned* breast of veal (6 lb before boning)	2 tablespoons lemon juice Spinach and Ham Filling	2 cans (13¾-oz size) chicken broth (3⅓ cups)
1¼ teaspoons salt	½ cup white wine	⅓ cup Madeira, ⅓ cup mayonnaise
¼ teaspoon pepper		
1 teaspoon dried thyme leaves	**GLAZE**	Cooked carrot slices
	2 env unflavored gelatine	Green pepper, capers

*Butcher will bone breast of veal; save bones for soup another day.
**If desired, veal may be served warm at this point with pan juices spooned over.

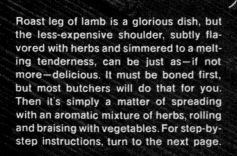

A DELICIOUS LAMB DISH

Roast leg of lamb is a glorious dish, but the less-expensive shoulder, subtly flavored with herbs and simmered to a melting tenderness, can be just as—if not more—delicious. It must be boned first, but most butchers will do that for you. Then it's simply a matter of spreading with an aromatic mixture of herbs, rolling and braising with vegetables. For step-by-step instructions, turn to the next page.

1 Wipe lamb with damp paper towels. Trim excess fat. Spread flat on board; pound with mallet to make even thickness. Pour lemon juice over lamb to cover completely. Filling: In bowl, combine chopped onion, parsley, salt, basil, marjoram and garlic; mix well.

3 In hot butter, brown roast evenly on all sides, turning with wooden spoons—takes about 25 minutes. Spoon off excess fat. Pour beef broth into a 2-cup measure. Add water to measure 1½ cups. Add to lamb along with bay leaf; bring to the boiling point.

5 Remove lamb, potatoes and onions to serving platter. Keep warm. Remove string from lamb; let stand 20 minutes for easier carving. Skim fat from pan liquid. Measure liquid; add water to make 1¾ cups. Mix flour with ¼ cup cold water until smooth.

2 Spread onion-parsley mixture evenly over lamb to within 1 inch of edge all around. Starting at short side, roll up; tie roll with string at 2-inch intervals to secure. If necessary, close ends with toothpicks. Slowly heat the butter in an 8-quart Dutch oven.

4 Reduce heat; simmer, covered, 1½ hours, turning meat at least once. Wash potatoes; pare strip around each one. Add potatoes and onions to Dutch oven. Simmer, covered, 40 minutes, or until lamb and vegetables are tender (test vegetables with a fork).

6 Stir into pan liquid; bring to boiling, stirring. Add chopped mint. Reduce heat, and simmer 3 minutes. Spoon some of mint gravy over meat, and pass the rest. Garnish serving platter with lemon slices and fresh mint leaves, if desired. Makes 8 to 10 servings.

POT ROAST OF LAMB

5½-lb boned* shoulder of lamb	1 teaspoon dried basil leaves	1 bay leaf
¼ cup lemon juice	½ teaspoon dried marjoram leaves	2 lb new potatoes (12)
FILLING	2 cloves garlic, crushed	8 medium onions, peeled
1 cup finely chopped onion	2 tablespoons butter or margarine	2 tablespoons flour
½ cup chopped parsley	1 can (10½ oz) condensed beef	½ cup chopped fresh
1½ teaspoons salt	broth, undiluted	mint leaves
*Have butcher bone lamb.		

1 Preheat oven to 325F. Place ham, fat side up, in shallow roasting pan. Place onion and bay leaves on ham; sprinkle with sugar, parsley, cloves, and peppers. Insert meat thermometer in center of thickest part, away

2 from bone. Pour beer into pan around ham. Cover pan tightly with foil. Bake, basting every 30 minutes with beer in pan, using a baster, about 3 hours, or until meat thermometer registers 130F. (Remove the ham from the oven;

3 take off foil; baste.) Make Glaze: When ham is done, remove it from roasting pan, and pour off all fat and drippings. Reserve 2 tablespoons of drippings (not fat); combine with brown sugar and honey. Return ham to roasting pan.

4 Increase oven temperature to 400F. With sharp knife, carefully remove any skin. To score: Make diagonal cuts in fat (be careful not to cut into meat), ¼ inch deep and 1¼ inches apart, using ruler, to form a diamond pattern.

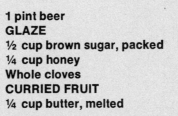

5 Stud the center of each diamond shape with a whole clove. To glaze the ham: Brush the surface with half of the honey glaze; return ham to oven, and bake 30 minutes longer, basting every 10 minutes with more of the glaze.

6 To make Curried Fruit: Mix butter, sugar, and curry. In 1½-quart casserole, toss fruit with sugar mixture. Bake, uncovered, 30 minutes in same oven. Serve along with ham. To carve ham, see below. Makes 20 servings.

INGREDIENTS

10- to 12-lb fully cooked
bone-in ham
1 cup sliced onion
2 bay leaves
¼ cup brown sugar, packed
4 sprigs parsley, 6 whole cloves
3 whole black peppers

1 pint beer
GLAZE
½ cup brown sugar, packed
¼ cup honey
Whole cloves
CURRIED FRUIT
¼ cup butter, melted

½ cup light-brown sugar,
packed
1 tablespoon curry powder
1 can (1 lb, 14 oz) peach
halves, drained
1 can (13¼ oz) pineapple
chunks, drained

SUMMER BAKED HAM

HOW TO CARVE IT

For easier carving, cool ham 20 minutes. Place so that bone end is at carver's right. From thin side of ham, cut 2 or 3 slices, parallel to length of ham, to make a flat surface. Turn ham to rest on cut surface. Cut small wedge-shape piece from shank end of ham; remove. With fork near wedge-shape cut steadying ham, make thin horizontal slices down to leg bone. Then run knife horizontally along bone to release slices. For more servings, turn ham back to original position, with fat side up.

Points To Remember: Most hams sold today are "fully cooked," but are at their best when further cooked to an internal temperature of 140F. "Cook before eating" hams must be cooked to 160F. Check label to identify the type of ham.

CASSEROLE, ITALIAN STYLE

Real Italian lasagna is definitely a dish to add to your
repertoire. It's great for entertaining—especially
this deluxe version, with both Italian sausage
and ground beef in the sauce. With lasagna,
serve antipasto and a green salad, Italian
bread, Chianti or beer, and fresh fruit for
dessert. The pasta should be cooked till
just tender, not soft—it will be cooked
more in the oven. A little oil in the
boiling water prevents sticking, and it's
easier to handle if you rinse it in
cold water after draining; then lay
it on paper towels to dry a little.

GEORGE RATKAI

1 Remove sausage meat from outer casings; chop the meat. In 5-quart Dutch oven, over medium heat, sauté sausage, beef (break up beef with wooden spoon), onion, and garlic, stirring frequently, until well browned—20 minutes. Add sugar, 1 tablespoon

2 salt, the basil, fennel, pepper, and half of parsley; mix well. Add tomatoes, tomato paste, and ½ cup water, mashing tomatoes with wooden spoon. Bring to boiling; reduce heat; simmer, covered and stirring occasionally, until thick—1½ hours. In 8-quart kettle,

3 bring 3 quarts water and 1 tablespoon salt to boiling. Add lasagna, 2 or 3 at a time. Return to boiling; boil, uncovered and stirring occasionally, 10 minutes, or just until tender. Drain in colander; rinse under cold water. Dry lasagna on paper towels. Preheat

4 oven to 375F. In medium bowl, combine ricotta, egg, remaining parsley, and salt; mix well. In bottom of 13-by-9-by-2-inch baking dish, spoon 1½ cups sauce. Layer with 6 lasagna, lengthwise and overlapping, to cover. Spread with half of ricotta mixture;

5 top with third of mozzarella. Spoon 1½ cups sauce over cheese; sprinkle with ¼ cup Parmesan. Repeat layering, starting with 6 lasagna and ending with 1½ cups sauce sprinkled with Parmesan. Spread with remaining sauce; top with rest of mozzarella

6 and Parmesan. Cover with foil, tucking around edge. Bake 25 minutes; remove foil; bake, uncovered, 25 minutes longer, or until bubbly. Cool 15 minutes before serving. To serve: With sharp knife, cut in squares. Use wide spatula to serve. Serves 8.

LASAGNA

1 lb sweet or hot Italian sausage (5 links)	½ teaspoon fennel seed	12 curly lasagna noodles (¾ of 1-lb pkg)
½ lb ground beef	¼ teaspoon pepper	1 container (15 oz) ricotta or cottage cheese, drained
½ cup finely chopped onion	¼ cup chopped parsley	1 egg, ½ teaspoon salt
2 cloves garlic, crushed	4 cups canned tomatoes, undrained; or 1 can (2 lb, 3 oz) Italian-style tomatoes	¾ lb mozzarella cheese, thinly sliced
2 tablespoons sugar		1 jar (3 oz) grated Parmesan cheese (¾ cup)
1 tablespoon salt	2 cans (6-oz size) tomato paste	
1½ teaspoons dried basil leaves	1 tablespoon salt	

Thousands of travelers to Greece and the Aegean return with appetites newly whetted for Greek food. A favorite is delicately flavored moussaka— a casserole of eggplant, ground lamb, tomato sauce, cheeses, and herbs. It's a complete meal, inexpensive and perfect for informal American entertaining. Beef lovers may prefer their moussaka made with ground chuck instead of lamb. Serve with green salad, hard rolls or Greek bread, and chilled white wine. Or, you might try retsina, the resin-flavored wine of Greece. Moussaka can be baked a day early, refrigerated, and reheated just in time for serving.

GEORGE RATKAI

A GIFT FROM THE GREEKS

1 Meat sauce: In hot butter in 3½-quart Dutch oven, sauté onion, chuck, garlic, stirring until brown—10 minutes. Add herbs, spices, tomato sauce; bring to boiling, stirring. Reduce heat; simmer, uncovered, ½ hour. Halve unpared eggplant lengthwise;

2 slice crosswise, ½ inch thick. Place in bottom of broiler pan; sprinkle lightly with salt; brush lightly with melted butter. Broil, 4 inches from heat, 4 minutes per side, or until golden. Make cream sauce: In medium saucepan, melt butter.

3 Remove from heat; stir in flour, salt, and pepper. Add milk gradually. Bring to boiling, stirring until mixture is thickened. Remove from heat. In small bowl, beat eggs with wire whisk. Beat in some hot cream-sauce mixture; return mixture

4 to saucepan; mix well; set aside. Preheat oven to 350F. To assemble casserole: In bottom of a shallow 2-quart baking dish (12 by 7½ by 2 inches, pictured), layer half of eggplant, overlapping slightly; sprinkle with 2 tablespoons each grated

5 Parmesan and Cheddar cheeses. Stir bread crumbs into meat sauce; spoon evenly over eggplant in casserole; then sprinkle with 2 tablespoons each Parmesan and Cheddar cheeses. Layer rest of eggplant slices, overlapping, as before.

6 Pour cream sauce over all. Sprinkle top with remaining cheese. Bake 35 to 40 minutes, or until golden-brown and top is set. If desired, brown top a little more under broiler—1 minute. Cool slightly to serve. Cut in squares. Makes 12 servings.

MOUSSAKA

MEAT SAUCE
2 tablespoons butter or margarine
1 cup finely chopped onion
1½ lb ground chuck or lamb
1 clove garlic, crushed
½ teaspoon dried oregano leaves
1 teaspoon dried basil leaves

½ teaspoon cinnamon
1 teaspoon salt
Dash pepper
2 cans (8-oz size) tomato sauce

2 eggplants (1-lb, 4-oz size), washed and dried
Salt
½ cup butter or margarine, melted

CREAM SAUCE
2 tablespoons butter or margarine
2 tablespoons flour
½ teaspoon salt, dash pepper
2 cups milk, 2 eggs

½ cup grated Parmesan cheese
½ cup grated Cheddar cheese
2 tablespoons dry bread crumbs

A cool idea for a special summer meal—chilled poached salmon in shimmering aspic. First, salmon steaks are simmered very slowly in a court bouillon—a delicately seasoned broth made with fresh vegetables, herbs and white wine. Fish should be cooked slowly over low heat; when it's just tender enough to separate easily with a fork, it's done. After poaching, salmon is cooled in the broth and refrigerated until well chilled. Then salmon is glazed and decorated with cucumber peel and olives.

CHILLED POACHED SALMON

1 In large skillet, combine ingredients for court bouillon with 1½ cups water. Bring to boiling. Reduce heat; simmer, covered, 15 minutes. Wash salmon under cold water; drain on paper towels. Add to skillet. Simmer, covered, 12 to 15 minutes.

2 Fish is cooked when it forms flakes easily when tested with fork. Set fish aside to cool in stock. Then refrigerate in stock 2 hours, to chill well. With slotted spatula, carefully remove salmon from skillet to wire rack, with a pan placed underneath to drain.

3 Reserve ½ cup fish stock. Using paring knife, carefully remove and discard skin. To make glaze: Sprinkle gelatine over ½ cup wine and ½ cup reserved fish stock in small saucepan; let stand 1 minute to soften. Stir over low heat to dissolve.

4 Set pan in bowl of ice cubes. Let stand, stirring occasionally, until gelatine is consistency of unbeaten egg white—about 10 minutes. Spoon some of gelatine mixture over salmon to glaze thinly. Cut olives and cucumber peel in strips and diamonds.

5 Arrange design on top with olive strips, cucumber stems and diamonds. Spoon rest of gelatine mixture over decoration to hold in place. If gelatine becomes too set, reheat and rechill. Reuse glaze from bottom of pan. Refrigerate until glaze is firm—about 1 hour.

6 Sauce verte: In blender, combine sauce ingredients; blend. Refrigerate, covered, in serving dish. To serve: With wide spatula, remove steaks to chilled platter. Garnish, as shown, with cucumber, watercress, lemon. Serve with sauce. Makes 4 servings.

SALMON STEAKS EN GELÉE

COURT BOUILLON
1½ cups dry white wine
1 small onion, sliced
1 carrot, pared and sliced
1 celery stalk, cut up
2 parsley sprigs
1 teaspoon salt
1 bay leaf
1 thin lemon slice

4 salmon steaks (¾ inch thick, about 2 lb)

GLAZE
1 env unflavored gelatine
½ cup dry white wine
½ cup fish stock
Pitted ripe olives
Cucumber peel

SAUCE VERTE
1 cup mayonnaise or cooked salad dressing
⅓ cup chopped fresh dill or watercress

⅓ cup chopped parsley
2 tablespoons capers, drained
1 tablespoon tarragon vinegar
1 tablespoon snipped chives

GARNISH
2 medium cucumbers, partially pared and sliced
Watercress or parsley
Lemon slices

GEORGE RATKAI

How to serve shrimp without ruining your budget? Curry it. Above, shrimp curry in the traditional Indian manner. When you add a generous bowl of saffron rice and all the trimmings—sliced bananas and cucumbers, peanuts, chopped peppers and tomatoes and pineapple chunks—

A CLASSIC SHRIMP CURRY

you'll find that two pounds of shrimp will feed six to eight people. Curry powder is not one but many spices, and Indians

mix their own. We buy it preblended, but it's easy to adjust the flavor to suit the food being curried with additional spices. To bring out the delicate taste of shrimp, we added extra cardamom and ginger, plus a touch of lime.

1 Curry sauce: In hot butter in large skillet, sauté onion, apple, garlic and curry—5 minutes. Remove from heat; blend in flour, 1 teaspoon salt, ¼ teaspoon each pepper, ginger and cardamom. Slowly add chicken and clam broths, lime juice and peel.

2 Bring to boiling, stirring constantly. Reduce heat; simmer, uncovered, 20 minutes, stirring occasionally. In saucepan, combine 1 quart water, 1 tablespoon salt, onion, lemon, parsley, peppercorns, bay leaf and thyme. Bring to boiling. Add shrimp.

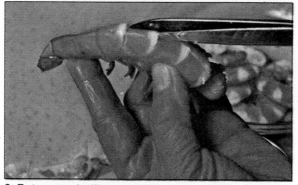

3 Return to boiling; reduce heat; simmer, uncovered, 4 minutes, or until tender when tested with fork (lift out one shrimp to test). Drain shrimp; discard liquid. Remove shell: With pointed scissors, cut the shell from head to tail down the back. Slip off shell.

4 With small knife, remove vein along back. Rinse shrimp under cold running water; drain well on paper towels. Set aside. Make saffron rice: In small bowl, mix saffron with 2 tablespoons hot water to dissolve the saffron as much as possible; set aside.

5 In hot butter in 5-quart Dutch oven, cook rice and salt, stirring occasionally, 5 minutes. Stir in the saffron mixture, then 3 cups water; bring to boiling. Reduce heat; simmer, tightly covered, 15 to 20 minutes, or until liquid is absorbed and rice is tender.

6 To serve: Add shrimp and chutney to sauce; heat gently for 10 minutes. Serve with saffron rice and curry accompaniments—sliced bananas, sliced cucumbers, peanuts, chopped tomatoes, chopped green pepper and pineapple chunks. Serves 6 to 8.

SHRIMP CURRY

CURRY SAUCE
¼ cup butter or margarine
1 cup chopped onion
1 cup chopped, pared tart apple
1 clove garlic, crushed
2 to 3 teaspoons curry powder
¼ cup unsifted all-purpose flour
Salt, pepper
Ground ginger and cardamom

1 can (10½ oz) condensed chicken broth, undiluted
2 cans (8-oz size) clam broth
2 tablespoons lime juice
2 teaspoons grated lime peel
1 tablespoon salt
1 small onion, sliced
6 lemon slices, 2 sprigs parsley
6 whole peppercorns

1 bay leaf
¼ teaspoon dried thyme leaves
2 lb raw shrimp in the shell
SAFFRON RICE
½ teaspoon crumbled saffron
¼ cup butter
1½ cups raw long-grain white rice
1½ teaspoons salt
⅓ cup chopped chutney

Definitely a company dish, this spectacular ring of sole filled with a delicate shrimp mousse looks and tastes like *haute cuisine*. But we have simplified and modernized its preparation so that any novice can make it successfully.

The shrimp mousse is made at the flick of a blender. The ring itself may be prepared and assembled the night before or in the morning, then refrigerated until dinner time and baked just before serving. Like all fish dishes, it must be cooked quickly, just until tender, and served at once. It's done when it flakes easily at the touch of a fork. (Fish turns tough and dry if overcooked.) Served with a green salad, it's the perfect conversation-making choice for a ladies' lunch, an informal supper, or as a first course for an elegant dinner party.

A SHRIMP MOUSSE WITH SOLE

GEORGE RATKAI

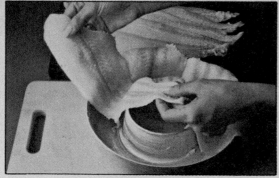

1 Rinse sole under cold water; dry on paper towels. Brush both sides with lemon juice; sprinkle with salt, pepper. Lightly butter a 5-cup ring mold (8½ inches across, 2 inches deep). Line mold with sole fillets, dark side up, narrow end to center, and overhanging the outside and inside rims.

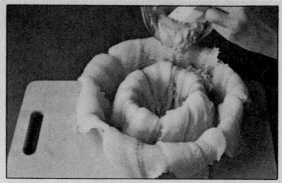

2 Make MOUSSE: Shell and de-vein shrimp; wash under cold water; drain well on paper towels; cut in half. Place in electric blender with egg whites, heavy cream, 1 teaspoon salt, the catsup, parsley, sherry. Blend at high speed, covered, 2 minutes, until smooth. Fill mold with mousse.

3 Preheat oven to 350F. Fold ends of fillets, overlapping, over top of filling. Using spatula, spread top with 1 tablespoon soft butter; cover top of mold loosely with a square of waxed paper. To bake: Place ring mold in 14-by-10-inch baking pan, then pour enough boiling water around

4 mold to measure 1 inch. Bake 30 minutes, or just until firm. Do not overbake. (Fish should flake easily when tested with fork.) While mold bakes, make SAUCE and sauté mushrooms. In double boiler top, over direct heat, melt ¼ cup butter; remove from heat. With wire whisk, blend in flour, salt;

5 gradually stir in light cream and catsup. Return to heat. Cook, over medium heat, stirring constantly, until mixture comes to a boil and thickens; simmer 1 minute. Remove from heat. In small bowl, with wire whisk, beat egg yolks; gradually beat in ½ cup of the hot sauce. Stir yolk mixture back into

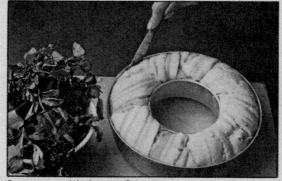

6 sauce; add sherry. Stir, over low heat, until hot. Keep warm over hot water in double boiler. With spatula, loosen edge of ring; pour off any liquid into sauce. Invert over heated platter; lift off mold. Spoon sauce over ring. Pass rest. Garnish with watercress, mushrooms, as pictured. Serves 6 to 8.

A SHRIMP MOUSSE WITH SOLE

8 sole fillets (2¼ lb) (see Note)	1 teaspoon salt	½ teaspoon salt
2 tablespoons lemon juice	1 tablespoon catsup	1 cup light cream
1 teaspoon salt	1 tablespoon chopped parsley	1 tablespoon catsup
⅛ teaspoon white pepper	2 tablespoons sherry	2 egg yolks
	1 tablespoon butter or margarine	½ cup dry sherry
SHRIMP MOUSSE		
1 lb raw shrimp	**SAUCE**	¼ lb mushrooms, thickly sliced,
2 egg whites	¼ cup butter or margarine	sautéed in 2 tablespoons butter
1 cup heavy cream	¼ cup flour	Watercress

Note: If using frozen sole or shrimp, thaw completely; drain well on paper towels before using.

Mousse of Sole and Veal Chaudfroid

Surprise luncheon or dinner guests with our delicate MOUSSE OF SOLE with lobster sauce. The surprise comes when you cut it and the sherry-rich sauce pours out— you poach the mousse with the sauce inside. VEAL CHAUDFROID makes a summer buffet a grand occasion. Stuffed with ham and spinach, the veal is cooked in wine, chilled and glazed with our simpler version of chaudfroid sauce—chicken-and-wine aspic blended with mayonnaise.

BREAST OF VEAL CHAUDFROID*

Spinach filling

1 pkg (10 oz) frozen chopped spinach
½ cup chopped parsley
¼ cup snipped chives

Cook spinach according to package directions: drain well on paper towels; combine with parsley and chives.

Ham filling

2 cups (1 lb) ground ham
2 tablespoons packaged dry bread crumbs
¼ teaspoon salt
Dash pepper
1 egg

In medium bowl, combine ham, bread crumbs, salt, pepper and egg; mix well.

*(See page 71 for Veal Chaudfroid recipe.)

1 Rinse sole; dry with paper towels. Cut each fillet into quarters; put through fine blade of meat grinder twice. Refrigerate, covered, ½ hour. Grease well a 2-quart metal charlotte mold (7 inches across); refrigerate. Filling: Heat butter in medium saucepan.

2 Remove from heat. Stir in ¼ cup flour and ¾ teaspoon salt. Gradually stir in 1 cup cream. Bring to boil, stirring; reduce heat; simmer 1 minute. With fork, beat yolks with ¼ cup cream. Stir into cream mixture, with sherry, mushrooms, catsup and lobster.

3 Cook, stirring, 1 minute. Mousse: To sole, add flour, salt, pepper; blend. With mixer at medium speed, beat in whites. Beat in cream, 2 tablespoons at a time—takes 10 minutes. Reserve 1 cup. Use rest to line bottom and side of mold to 1 inch of top.

4 Preheat oven to 325F. Refrigerate 1 cup lobster filling. Fill lined mold with rest of filling. Cover with the 1 cup reserved sole mixture, spreading to edge of mold. Cover top of mold loosely with greased waxed paper. Place mold in a shallow roasting pan.

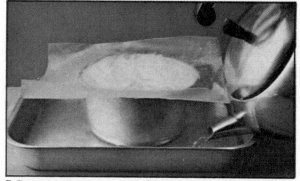

5 Pour boiling water to 2-inch level around mold. Bake 45 to 50 minutes, or until firm at edge when gently pressed with fingertip. Sauce: About 10 minutes before mousse is done, heat reserved lobster filling in top of double boiler over hot water.

6 Stir in 2 to 3 tablespoons sherry to thin mixture. To serve: Loosen mousse around side with small spatula. Invert onto heated serving platter; lift off mold. Spoon some of heated filling over top; serve with rest of filling as a sauce. Makes 8 servings.

MOUSSE OF SOLE WITH LOBSTER SAUCE

1½ lb sole fillets (not frozen)

LOBSTER FILLING AND SAUCE
3 tablespoons butter, ¼ cup flour
¾ teaspoon salt
1¼ cups light cream

2 egg yolks, ⅓ cup dry sherry
1 can(3oz)whole mushrooms,drained
1 tablespoon catsup
2 cups cubed cooked
lobster (see Note)

MOUSSE
¼ cup flour, 1½ teaspoons salt
⅛ teaspoon white pepper
2 egg whites (⅓ cup)
1¾ cups light cream, dry sherry

Note: In 3-quart saucepan, bring 1½ quarts water to boiling, with ½ small onion, sliced; ½ lemon, sliced; ½ tablespoon salt; 3 black peppercorns and 1 small bay leaf. Drop in 3 (8-ounce size) frozen rock-lobster tails. Bring back to boiling; reduce heat; simmer, covered, 9 minutes. Remove lobster tails; let cool.

MAN, OH, MANICOTTI, WHAT A PASTA!

Manicotti (the word means "little muffs") is a Southern Italian favorite—tubes of pasta stuffed with cheese and served with a savory tomato sauce. Usually, here in this country, the dish is made with packaged manicotti shells, but there's a better way. You can make your own manicotti shells much as you would make pancakes or crepes. **Points to Remember:** Beat batter for shells just until well mixed; it shouldn't be frothy. Let stand a half hour or so before using—or even overnight in the refrigerator. Cook manicotti in a nonstick skillet—otherwise, you'll need to oil the pan from time to time. You can make shells and sauce a day in advance, and refrigerate. Next page, step-by-step recipe for two casseroles (one to cook, one to freeze). Each serves six.

1 Make Sauce: In hot oil in 5-quart Dutch oven, sauté onion and garlic 5 minutes. Mix in rest of sauce ingredients and 1½ cups water, mashing tomatoes with fork. Bring to boiling, and reduce heat. Simmer mixture, covered and stirring occasionally, 1 hour.

2 Make Manicotti: In medium bowl, combine 6 eggs, the flour, ¼ teaspoon salt, and 1½ cups water; with electric mixer, beat just until smooth. Let stand ½ hour or longer. Slowly heat an 8-inch skillet * Pour in 3 tablespoons batter, rotating the skillet quickly

3 to spread batter evenly over bottom. Cook over medium heat until top is dry but bottom is not brown. Turn out on a wire rack to cool. Continue cooking until all of the batter is used. As the manicotti cool, stack them with waxed paper between them.

4 Preheat oven to 350F. Make Filling: In large bowl, combine ricotta, mozzarella, ⅓ cup Parmesan, the eggs, salt, pepper, and parsley; beat with wooden spoon to blend well. Spread about ¼ cup filling down the center of each manicotti, and roll up.

5 Spoon 1½ cups sauce into each of two 12-by-8-by-2-inch baking dishes. Place eight rolled manicotti, seam side down, in single layer; top with five more. Cover with 1 cup sauce; sprinkle with Parmesan. Bake, uncovered, ½ hour, or until bubbly.

6 To freeze: Line baking dish with large piece of foil; assemble as directed. Fold foil over to seal, and freeze in dish. When frozen, remove dish. To serve: Unwrap; place in baking dish, and let stand 1 hour to thaw. Bake, covered, 1 hour in 350F oven.

BAKED MANICOTTI WITH CHEESE FILLING

SAUCE: ⅓ cup olive or salad oil	1 teaspoon dried oregano leaves	1 pkg (8 oz) mozzarella cheese, diced
1½ cups finely chopped onion	1 teaspoon dried basil leaves	⅓ cup grated Parmesan cheese
1 clove garlic, crushed	¼ teaspoon pepper	
1 can (2 lb, 3 oz) Italian tomatoes, undrained	**MANICOTTI: 6 eggs,** at room temperature	2 eggs, 1 teaspoon salt
1 can (6 oz) tomato paste	1½ cups unsifted all-purpose	¼ teaspoon pepper
2 tablespoons chopped parsley	flour, ¼ teaspoon salt	1 tablespoon chopped parsley
1 tablespoon salt	**FILLING: 2 lb ricotta cheese**	¼ cup grated Parmesan cheese
1 tablespoon sugar		

*If not using a skillet with a non-stick surface, brush skillet lightly with butter for each manicotti.

This glamorous puffy omelet, light and delicate as a soufflé, is substantial enough to serve as a main dish for lunch or supper. It's economical, too. Made with six eggs, it serves four to six people. There's a trick to making it puff: Let egg whites warm to room temperature before beating them to give maximum volume. Serve with a rich cheese sauce, a seafood sauce or a Spanish-style tomato sauce. A green vegetable and light dessert completes the meal. Step-by-step instructions are on the following page.

THE PERFECT PUFFY OMELET

1 Separate whites into large bowl, yolks into small bowl. Let whites warm to room temperature 1 hour. Preheat oven to 350F. With portable mixer at high speed, beat whites with cream of tartar just until stiff peaks form when beater is slowly raised.

2 Using same beater, beat yolks until thick and lemon-colored. Add salt, mustard and pepper. Gradually add milk; beat until blended. With wire whisk or rubber scraper, using an under-and-over motion, gently fold yolk mixture into whites just to combine.

3 Slowly heat a 10- or 11-inch heavy skillet with a heat-resistant handle. Test temperature: Sprinkle with a little cold water; it will roll off in drops. Heat oil and butter to sizzling—don't brown; tilt pan to coat side. Spread egg mixture evenly in pan.

4 Cook over low heat, without stirring, until lightly browned on underside—about 2 minutes. Transfer skillet to oven; bake, uncovered, 15 minutes, or until golden-brown and top seems firm when gently pressed with finger. Meanwhile, make Cheese Sauce.

5 In small saucepan, melt butter; remove from heat. Stir in flour, mustard, salt, pepper, cayenne and milk until smooth. Bring to boiling, stirring until thickened. Reduce heat; add the grated cheese; cook, stirring, until cheese is melted and mixture is smooth.

6 With a knife, make a cut, 1 inch deep, slightly to right of center of omelet. Fold smaller part over larger part. Turn out onto heated platter, loosening with spatula. Spoon sauce over omelet. Sprinkle with paprika. Garnish with parsley. Makes 4 servings.

OMELET

6 egg whites (¾ cup)
6 egg yolks
¼ teaspoon cream of tartar
¾ teaspoon salt
½ teaspoon dry mustard
Dash pepper
⅓ cup milk
2 teaspoons salad oil

2 tablespoons butter or margarine

CHEESE SAUCE
2 tablespoons butter or margarine
2 tablespoons flour
½ teaspoon dry mustard

¾ teaspoon salt
Dash pepper
Dash cayenne
1 cup milk
1 cup grated sharp Cheddar cheese (¼ lb)
Paprika
Parsley sprigs

GEORGE RATKAI

BLINTZES—THE DIETER'S DOWNFALL

Golden pancakes filled with creamy cheese and topped with jam and sour cream, blintzes belong to that select group of dishes capable of melting the willpower of even the strictest dieter. And they're wonderfully versatile. Serve them for brunch or supper—the cheese provides plenty of protein—or have them for dessert. Cheese is the classic filling, but you can also make blueberry blintzes, strawberry blintzes, even apple blintzes. Best of all, you can make and fill them several hours in advance. Simply refrigerate, then sauté just before serving. Step by step directions, next page.

1 Make batter: In medium bowl, with portable electric mixer or rotary beater, beat eggs, salad oil and milk to blend well. Add flour and salt; continue to beat until batter is smooth and flour is dissolved. Refrigerate, covered, 30 minutes, or until ready to use.

2 Make cheese filling: In medium bowl, combine egg yolk and granulated sugar; beat with portable electric mixer until thick and yellow. Add cheeses and vanilla; stir until well combined. Makes 3 cups. Refrigerate until ready to use. Slowly heat an 8-inch skillet.

3 To test temperature, drop a little cold water onto hot skillet; water should roll off in drops. For each blintz, brush inside of pan lightly with melted butter. Measure 3 tablespoons batter into ¼ cup. Pour in all at once, rotating skillet quickly to spread evenly.

4 Batter should be like heavy cream. If it seems too thick, dilute with a little milk. Cook until golden on underside—1 minute; remove, loosening edge with spatula. Dry on paper towels. Stack, browned side up, with waxed paper between blintzes. Makes 16.

5 To fill: Spread 3 level tablespoons filling on browned side of each blintz, making rectangle 4 inches long. Fold two opposite sides over filling; then overlap ends, covering filling completely. Melt 1 tablespoon butter in large skillet over medium heat.

6 Add half of blintzes, not touching, seam side down; sauté until golden-brown on underside; turn; sauté other side. Keep warm in a low oven while cooking rest. Serve hot, sprinkled with confectioners' sugar, with sour cream and preserves. Serves 8.

BLINTZES

3 eggs
3 tablespoons salad oil
1½ cups milk
1 cup unsifted all-purpose flour
½ teaspoon salt
⅓ cup butter or margarine,
melted

CHEESE FILLING
1 egg yolk
2 tablespoons granulated sugar
1 pkg (8 oz) cream cheese,
softened
2 cups (1 lb) creamed
cottage cheese

¼ teaspoon vanilla extract
2 tablespoons butter or
margarine
Confectioners' sugar
1 cup sour cream
1 cup strawberry or cherry
preserves

GEORGE RATKAI

McCall's Cooking School:
The Rise of the Soufflé

Soufflés are among the trickiest dishes in a cook's repertoire. For this reason, we are launching McCall's Cooking School with the step-by-step secrets for making the elegant chocolate soufflé shown at left. Follow the steps, and it will turn out puffy and perfect every time. The purpose of the school is to show you, in pictures and words, the precise procedures and technical tricks used in preparing special dishes—the kind of tricks you might learn in private lessons, but which recipes rarely spell out. And, in addition to the "how," we give you the "why"—the reasons behind an expert cook's maneuvers—so you can apply these techniques in other recipes.

CHEF'S NOTES ON SOUFFLÉS

1. Eggs are easier to separate when cold; a fresh yolk is less apt to break.

2. Never break eggs over a large bowl of whites. If the yolk breaks, all of the whites will be ruined. Separate whites, one by one, into a small bowl, turning each into large bowl.

3. Egg whites will not beat up to full volume if there's even a tiny bit of yolk (or anything of a fatty nature) in them or on the bowl or beaters. If any egg yolk does get into whites, try removing it with a small piece of paper towel.

4. Egg whites have better volume if slightly warm when beaten; let stand at room temperature about an hour.

5. Waxed-paper collar lets soufflé rise above dish and hold its shape.

6. The inside of the dish and paper are sprinkled with sugar to make a rough surface for the rising soufflé to adhere to.

7. In cooking the chocolate mixture over direct heat, be careful that it does not scorch. (Chocolate burns easily.) Stir often, and remove from heat as soon as it is thickened.

8. In combining egg yolks with a hot mixture, stir a little of the hot mixture into yolks so that they change tempera-ture gradually. Then gradually stir egg yolks into rest of hot mixture. They may curdle if combined all at once.

9. In folding the cooled, cooked mixture into the beaten egg whites, be careful not to break down the egg whites. It is the air beaten into the egg whites that expands from the heat of the oven and gives volume to the soufflé. Loss of air means loss of volume.

10. The soufflé is baked in a pan of hot water as this permits it to rise more slowly and evenly. If necessary, the soufflé may remain in the oven in the hot water, with the heat turned off, 10 minutes or so after it is baked, if it cannot be served at once.

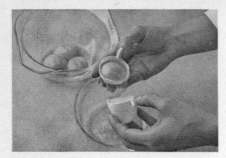

1 Separate eggs: Crack shell, keeping yolk in one half, white in other. Turn yolk from one half into the other, letting white run into a small bowl, yolk into another. Pour each white into large bowl; let stand to warm 1 hour

2 With 1 tablespoon butter, grease 2-quart soufflé dish. Fold 26-inch piece waxed paper lengthwise in thirds. Grease with 1 tablespoon butter. Form 2-inch collar around dish; tie. Sprinkle dish, paper with 2 tablespoons sugar

3 In medium-size, heavy saucepan, with wire whisk, mix flour, cocoa, ¾ cup granulated sugar, the salt. Gradually blend in milk. Cook, stirring, over medium heat, until mixture comes to boil (large bubbles break on surface)

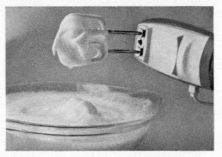

4 Beat yolks with a wire whisk. Beat in some of cocoa mixture. Gradually stir yolk mixture into rest of mixture in saucepan. Add 2 tablespoons butter and the vanilla, stirring until they are combined. Set aside to cool slightly

5 Add cream of tartar to egg whites. With electric mixer at high speed, beat just until soft peaks form when beater is slowly raised; scrape side of bowl several times with rubber scraper so that egg whites are beaten throughout

6 Add ¼ cup granulated sugar, 2 tablespoons at a time, beating well after each addition. Beat just until stiff peaks form when beater is raised. Whites will be shiny and satiny. Turn a third of cocoa mixture over top of

7 egg whites. Using a wire whisk or rubber scraper, gently fold mixture into whites, using under-and-over motion, just until combined. Fold in rest of cocoa mixture a half at a time. Caution: Overfolding reduces the volume

8 Using a rubber scraper, gently turn soufflé mixture, without stirring, into prepared dish set in a large baking pan; clean out bowl with scraper. Smooth top with a metal spatula. Place pan and dish in oven on bottom rack

9 Pour hot water into pan to measure 1 inch. Bake 1¼ hours. With rotary beater, beat cream with confectioners' sugar until stiff. Chill. To serve, remove collar. Break the top of the soufflé with fork. Serve with whipped cream

CHOCOLATE SOUFFLÉ

8 egg whites	½ cup all-purpose flour	2 cups milk
6 egg yolks	¾ cup Dutch-process	1 teaspoon vanilla extract
4 tablespoons butter or regular	unsweetened cocoa	¼ teaspoon cream of tartar
margarine, softened	1 cup granulated sugar	1 cup heavy cream, chilled
2 tablespoons granulated sugar	¼ teaspoon salt	¼ cup confectioners' sugar

Preheat oven to 350F. Place oven rack on lowest rung in oven. Start with step 1, above.

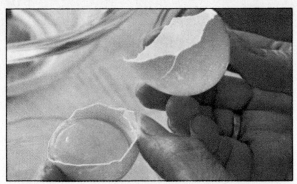

1 Separate eggs—whites into one large bowl and yolks into another. Let whites warm to room temperature—1 hour. Butter a 1½-quart, straight-sided soufflé dish (7½ inches in diameter). Dust lightly with grated Parmesan cheese—about 1 tablespoon.

2 Fold a sheet of waxed paper, 26 inches long lengthwise into thirds. Lightly butter one side. Wrap waxed paper around soufflé dish, with buttered side against dish and a 2-inch rim extending above top edge to make a collar. Tie with string.

3 Preheat oven to 350F. Melt 5 tablespoons butter in medium saucepan; remove from heat. Using a wire whisk or wooden spoon, stir in flour, 1 teaspoon salt and the cayenne until smooth. Gradually stir in milk. Bring to boiling, stirring constantly.

4 Reduce heat; simmer, stirring, until mixture is thick and leaves bottom and side of pan. Beat egg yolks with wire whisk or wooden spoon. Gradually beat cooked mixture into yolks. Beat in ½ cup Parmesan cheese and the grated Swiss cheese.

5 At high speed, beat whites with ½ teaspoon salt and the cream of tartar until stiff peaks form when beater is slowly raised. With wire whisk, using an under-and-over motion, gently fold one third of whites into warm cheese mixture to combine well.

6 Carefully fold in remaining egg whites just until combined. Turn into prepared soufflé dish. Bake 40 minutes, or until soufflé is puffed and golden-brown. Carefully remove collar just before serving. Serve soufflé at once. Makes 4 servings.

FABULOUS CHEESE SOUFFLÉ

6 eggs	6 tablespoons unsifted	1¼ cups milk
Butter or regular	all-purpose flour	½ cup coarsely grated
margarine	1½ teaspoons salt	natural Swiss cheese
Grated Parmesan cheese	Dash cayenne	¼ teaspoon cream of tartar

A soufflé must come to the table straight from the oven the very moment it is ready—it cannot wait for guests. To remove any risks, we suggest preparing the soufflé up to the point of baking. Refrigerate it until guests have arrived (it will keep up to 4 hours). Then, while cocktails are being served, remove to oven and bake as directed, increasing baking time by 10 to 15 minutes, since soufflé will be cold.

A VERY SPECIAL SOUFFLÉ

Our delicate soufflé is a light and refreshing way to conclude a good meal. The sweet yet tart savor of dried apricots gives it a very special flavor. What's more, the ingredients can be combined ahead of time, refrigerated and popped into the oven just as everyone is sitting down to dinner. Fifty minutes later, it's ready to serve—in a soufflé dish or, as shown, unmolded and topped with apricot preserves. Directions on next page.

1 Let egg whites warm to room temperature in large bowl of electric mixer at least one hour to give more volume. Meanwhile, in medium saucepan, combine dried apricots with 1¼ cups water; bring to boiling. Remove from heat; let stand, covered, 20 minutes.

2 Puree apricots and liquid in blender or press through food mill. Puree will measure 1½ cups. Add almond extract; turn into large bowl. Preheat oven to 350F. Lightly butter inside of 3-quart mold or pyrex bowl. Sprinkle evenly with 2 to 3 tablespoons sugar.

3 Add cream of tartar and salt to egg whites; beat at high speed just until soft peaks form when beater is slowly raised. Then gradually beat in 1 cup granulated sugar, 2 tablespoons at a time, beating well after each addition. Continue to beat at high speed.

4 Beat until very stiff peaks form when beater is slowly raised. With wire whisk, using an under-and-over motion, gently fold one third of egg whites into puree to combine well. Fold in rest of egg whites just to combine. Do not overmix. Turn into mold.

5 Set in pan containing 1 inch hot water. On low shelf in oven, bake 50 minutes, or until puffed and golden-brown. Meanwhile, beat cream with 2 tablespoons confectioners' sugar just until stiff. Turn into serving bowl; refrigerate to chill very well.

6 Melt preserves in small skillet; strain, if desired. To unmold soufflé, loosen around edge of mold with small spatula; invert on warm serving platter. Shake gently to release. Lift off mold. Brush melted preserves over top. Serve with whipped cream. Serves 8.

MOLDED APRICOT SOUFFLE

8 egg whites (1⅓ cups)
1 cup dried apricots, packed, about 36 (6 oz)
½ teaspoon almond extract

2 tablespoons butter
or margarine
Granulated sugar
½ teaspoon cream of tartar

½ teaspoon salt
1 cup heavy cream
Confectioners' sugar
½ cup apricot preserves

DESSERTS

A VERY SPECIAL CAKE

A torte is no ordinary cake, and our chocolate-nut torte is no everyday dessert. It's for great occasions—holidays, birthdays and other special celebrations. The classic torte is a light, airy, sponge-type cake with one to 12 layers—ours has three. We've put them together with a luscious whipped-cream filling and topped it all with chocolate frosting. The layers, rich with ground pecans and hazelnuts, get their delicate texture from beaten egg whites. Bread crumbs are used in place of flour.

Layers may be made ahead of time and frozen, then thawed and filled for serving.

1 Separate eggs, putting whites into large electric-mixer bowl, yolks into small one. Let whites warm to room temperature—about 1 hour. Preheat oven to 375F. Line bottom of 3 (8-inch) round layer-cake pans with circles of waxed paper. With mixer at

2 high speed, beat whites with ¼ teaspoon salt until soft peaks form when beater is slowly raised. Gradually beat in ½ cup granulated sugar (2 tablespoons at a time), beating until stiff peaks form. With same beaters, beat yolks until thick and light. Gradually beat

3 in rest of granulated sugar, beating until thick—3 minutes; beat in 1 teaspoon vanilla. Combine ground nuts, crumbs, baking powder, and salt; turn into yolk mixture. With rubber scraper, mix well; with under-and-over motion, fold into whites just to combine.

4 Divide evenly into prepared pans, smoothing surfaces. Bake 25 minutes, or until surface springs back when gently pressed with fingertip. To cool, hang each pan upside down between 2 other pans—1 hour. Make filling: In medium bowl, combine the cream,

5 ½ cup confectioners' sugar, and 1 teaspoon vanilla. Beat until stiff; refrigerate. Frosting: In top of double boiler, over hot water, melt chocolate, butter. Remove from water; mix in sugar, hot water, vanilla until smooth. Loosen sides of layers from pans with

6 spatula. Turn out of pans; peel off paper. On plate, assemble layers, with half of filling between each two. Put 1 cup frosting in pastry bag with number-2 star tip; refrigerate. Frost torte; decorate as pictured. For easier cutting, refrigerate 1 hour. Serves 12.

CHOCOLATE-NUT TORTE

TORTE LAYERS
7 eggs
¼ teaspoon salt
1 cup granulated sugar
1 teaspoon vanilla extract
1¼ cups ground hazelnuts
(10 oz unshelled)
1¼ cups ground pecans
(10 oz unshelled)

¼ cup packaged dry bread crumbs
1 teaspoon baking powder
½ teaspoon salt

FILLING
1 cup heavy cream, chilled
½ cup confectioners' sugar
1 teaspoon vanilla extract

FROSTING
4 squares unsweetened chocolate
¼ cup butter or regular margarine
3 cups sifted confectioners' sugar
½ cup hot water or coffee
1½ teaspoons vanilla extract
Whole hazelnuts and pecans

THE PERFECT CHOCOLATE CAKE

We're going to come right out and say it: This is the most delicious chocolate cake you ever tasted! Moist, light, sinfully rich, made with cocoa, lots of chocolate, and whipped cream, it can't be found in a bakery or made from a cake mix. Follow our recipe exactly—accurate measurements, no substitutions, the right pan size—and you'll have a perfect dessert that you (and we) can really be proud of. Instructions on opposite page.

1 In medium bowl, combine cocoa with boiling water, mixing with wire whisk until smooth. Cool completely. Sift flour with soda, salt, and baking powder. Preheat oven to 350F. Grease well and lightly flour three 9-by-1½-inch layer-cake pans.

2 In large bowl of electric mixer, at high speed, beat butter, sugar, eggs, and vanilla, scraping bowl occasionally, until light—about 5 minutes. At low speed, beat in flour mixture (in fourths), alternately with cocoa mixture (in thirds), beginning

3 and ending with flour mixture. Do not overbeat. Divide evenly into pans; smooth top. Bake 25 to 30 minutes, or until surface springs back when gently pressed with fingertip. Cool in pans 10 minutes. Carefully loosen sides with spatula; remove

4 from pans; cool on racks. Frosting: In medium saucepan, combine chocolate pieces, cream, butter; stir over medium heat until smooth. Remove from heat. With whisk, blend in 2½ cups confectioners' sugar. In bowl set over ice, beat until it

5 holds shape. Filling: Whip cream with sugar and vanilla; refrigerate. To assemble cake: On plate, place a layer, top side down; spread with half of cream. Place second layer, top side down; spread with rest of cream. Place third layer, top side

6 up. To frost: With spatula, frost sides first, covering whipped cream; use rest of frosting on top, swirling decoratively. Refrigerate at least 1 hour before serving. To cut, use a thin-edged sharp knife; slice with a sawing motion. Serves 10 to 12.

PERFECT CHOCOLATE CAKE

CAKE
1 cup unsifted unsweetened
  cocoa
2 cups boiling water
2¾ cups sifted
  all-purpose flour
2 teaspoons baking soda
½ teaspoon salt
½ teaspoon baking powder

1 cup butter or regular
  margarine, softened
2½ cups granulated sugar
4 eggs
1½ teaspoons vanilla extract
FROSTING
1 pkg (6 oz) semisweet
  chocolate pieces
½ cup light cream

1 cup butter or regular
  margarine
2½ cups unsifted
  confectioners' sugar
FILLING
1 cup heavy cream, chilled
¼ cup unsifted confectioners'
  sugar
1 teaspoon vanilla extract

BAKE A YULE LOG

No French Christmas celebration would be complete without a *bûche de Noël,* the traditional Christmas cake baked and decorated to look like a Yule log. This is an American version, perfect as dessert for a dinner party, decorative on a holiday buffet table or an ideal choice if you're serving just dessert and coffee during the holidays. And it's much easier to make than it looks. Actually, it's very much like a jelly roll—the cake is rolled around a rich, creamy filling and then decorated. The cake itself is a light, cocoa-flavored sponge, baked flat in a jelly-roll pan. The filling is rich, mocha whipped cream. The entire cake is sprinkled with confectioners' sugar, to give the illusion of snow, and decorated with red and green candied angelica and cherries. You can, if you wish, vary the filling. For a children's party, for instance, you might fill it with ice cream—pistachio, perhaps, or peppermint stick—for one more touch of Christmas green or red.

1 Grease bottom of a 15½-by-10½-by-1-inch jelly-roll pan; line with waxed paper; grease lightly. Preheat the oven to 375F. In a large electric-mixer bowl, at high speed, beat egg whites just until soft peaks form when the beater is slowly raised.

2 Add ¼ cup sugar, 2 tablespoons at a time, beating until stiff peaks form when beater is slowly raised. With same beaters, beat yolks at high speed, adding remaining ½ cup sugar, 2 tablespoons at a time. Beat until mixture is very thick—about 4 minutes.

3 At low speed, beat in cocoa, vanilla and salt, just until smooth. With wire whisk or rubber scraper, using an under-and-over motion, gently fold the cocoa mixture into the beaten egg whites, just until they are blended (no egg white should show).

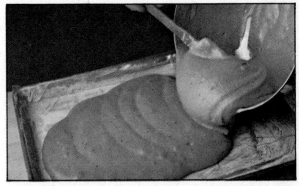

4 Spread evenly in pan. Bake 15 minutes, just until surface springs back when gently pressed with fingertip. Sift confectioners' sugar, in a 15-by-10-inch rectangle, on clean linen towel. Turn cake out on sugar; lift off pan; peel paper off cake.

5 Roll up, jelly-roll fashion, starting with the short end, towel and all. Cool completely on rack, seam side down—at least ½ hour. To make the filling: Combine ingredients in medium bowl. Beat with electric mixer until thick, and then refrigerate.

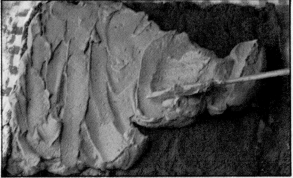

6 Unroll cake; spread with filling to 1 inch from edge; reroll. Place, seam side down, on plate; cover loosely with foil. Refrigerate 1 hour before serving. To serve: Sprinkle with confectioners' sugar; decorate with angelica and cherries. Serves 10.

HOLIDAY CHOCOLATE LOG

6 egg whites (see Note)	Confectioners' sugar	¼ cup unsweetened cocoa
¾ cup sugar, 6 egg yolks		2 teaspoons instant coffee
⅓ cup unsweetened cocoa	**FILLING**	1 teaspoon vanilla extract
1½ teaspoons vanilla extract	1½ cups heavy cream, chilled	
Dash salt	½ cup confectioners' sugar	Candied cherries, angelica

Note: Let egg whites warm to room temperature—about 1 hour. You may make the Chocolate Log a week ahead, then freeze it, wrapped in foil. Let stand at room temperature to thaw for about 1 hour before serving.

DIETER'S DELIGHT

Fluffy, light-as-a-feather angel-food cake is sheer heaven for dieters. It's by far the lowest in calories of all cakes—since the main ingredient is egg whites beaten to a froth. Whether you're dieting or not, serve it often—either plain, or with ice cream, sherbet or with fresh fruit.

1 Separate eggs while still cold from the refrigerator. Measure whites; pour into large bowl of electric mixer to warm to room temperature—about 1 hour. Sift flour; measure, then sift with ¾ cup sugar; resift three times. Preheat the oven to 375F.

2 At medium speed, beat whites with salt and cream of tartar just until soft peaks form when beater is slowly raised. Do not overbeat. (Bowl, beaters, wire whisk and rubber scraper must be free of any grease as it retards beating of egg whites.)

3 At high speed, gradually beat in 1 cup sugar, ¼ cup at a time, beating well after each addition. Continue beating until stiff peaks form when beater is slowly raised. With wire whisk or rubber scraper, gently fold extracts into whites to combine.

4 Sprinkle one fourth of flour mixture over whites. With wire whisk, using an under-and-over motion, gently fold flour mixture into whites (about 15 strokes), rotating bowl a quarter turn after each stroke, folding just until flour mixture disappears.

5 Continue folding in flour mixture, one fourth at a time, as in step 4. With rubber scraper, gently push batter into an ungreased 10-inch tube pan. With knife, cut through batter twice to remove any large air bubbles. Spread evenly, to smooth the top.

6 Bake on lowest rack in oven 30 to 35 minutes, or until top springs back when gently pressed with finger. Invert pan over neck of bottle to cool completely—2 hours. With knife, loosen cake from side of pan; turn out. Serve right side up. Serves 12.

ANGEL-FOOD CAKE

1¾ cups egg whites
(12 to 14 whites,
depending on
size of the eggs)

1¼ cups sifted cake flour
(sift before measuring)
1¾ cups granulated sugar
½ teaspoon salt

1½ teaspoons cream of
tartar
1 teaspoon vanilla extract
½ teaspoon almond extract

Note: To get good volume, let egg whites warm to room temperature before beating them. Be sure to use cake (not all-purpose) flour in this recipe. If you are baking the cake a day ahead, leave it in the pan and remove it just before serving. Cut cake with a knife with a serrated edge, using a light sawing motion.

Our light and lemony daffodil cake is really two cakes in one—a golden, rich spongecake and a delicate angel-food cake. The batters are made separately and swirled together into marble cake right in the baking pan. What's more, it's

A LIGHT AND LEMONY CAKE

one of the least expensive cakes you can bake. The basic ingredients are flour, sugar and eggs—and the absence of butter makes this recipe a boon for dieters. The cake will stay fresh and moist for days. Instructions, next page.

1 Make white batter: In large bowl, let whites warm to room temperature 1 hour. Sift 1¼ cups flour with ½ cup sugar; resift three times. With electric mixer at high speed, beat whites with salt and cream of tartar until soft peaks form when beater is slowly raised.

2 Beat in 1 cup sugar, ¼ cup at a time, beating well after each addition. Beat until stiff peaks form when beater is slowly raised. With wire whisk, fold vanilla into egg whites until combined. Sift flour mixture, one fourth at a time, over egg whites.

3 With wire whisk, using an under-and-over motion, gently fold in each addition with 15 strokes, rotating bowl a quarter of a turn after each addition. Fold ten more strokes, to blend completely. Turn one third batter into medium bowl. Preheat oven to 375F.

4 Make yellow batter: In small bowl, combine yolks, cake flour and sugar. With mixer at high speed, beat until very thick. Add lemon peel. With wire whisk, using an under-and-over motion, fold yolk mixture into reserved one third batter with 15 strokes.

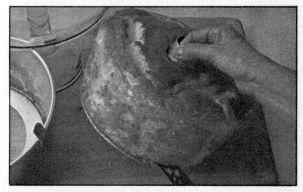

5 For marbling, spoon batters alternately into an ungreased 10-inch tube pan, ending with white batter on top. With knife, cut through batter twice. With rubber scraper, gently spread batter in pan until it is smooth on top and touches side of pan all around.

6 Bake on lower oven rack 35 to 40 minutes, or until cake springs back when pressed with fingertip. Invert pan over neck of bottle to cool 2 hours. With spatula, loosen cake from pan; remove. Sprinkle with confectioners' sugar, if desired. Serves 10.

McCALL'S BEST DAFFODIL CAKE

WHITE BATTER
1¾ cups egg whites (12 to 14)
1¼ cups sifted cake flour
(sift before measuring)
1½ cups sugar
½ teaspoon salt

1½ teaspoons cream of tartar
1½ teaspoons vanilla extract

YELLOW BATTER
5 egg yolks
2 tablespoons cake flour

2 tablespoons sugar
2 tablespoons grated lemon peel

Confectioners' sugar

Note: To get good volume, let egg whites warm to room temperature before beating them. Be sure to use cake (not all-purpose) flour in this recipe. If you are baking the cake a day ahead, leave it in the pan overnight, and remove it just before serving. Cut cake with a knife with a serrated edge, using a light, sawing motion. Nice served with ice cream.

McCALL'S COOKING SCHOOL

In the old days, a poundcake was literally a "pound cake"—it took a pound of butter, a pound of eggs, a pound of sugar, a pound of flour, and considerable culinary skill to make one. Consequently, poundcake was a special treat, to be saved for special occasions. A perfect poundcake is still a special treat, but the old rule of thumb has given way to a more scientific blend of ingredients, and a perfect cake depends more on a good recipe than great culinary skill. Here is our best poundcake recipe.

Ingredients for Cake: 8 egg whites (1 cup), 3 cups sifted all-purpose flour, 1 teaspoon baking powder, salt, 2 cups granulated sugar, 8 egg yolks, 2 cups butter or regular margarine (4 sticks), 1 tablespoon grated orange peel, 2 tablespoons grated lemon peel, and 2 tablespoons lemon juice.

Ingredients for Glaze: 1 tablespoon butter, 1 package (1 pound) confectioners' sugar, 1 teaspoon grated lemon peel, and ⅓ cup lemon juice.

First, separate eggs, turning yolks into one large bowl and whites into another. Let egg whites warm to room temperature—about 1 hour. Preheat oven to 350F.

POUNDCAKE: PENNY-WISE AND POUND-WISE, TOO

1 With a little shortening, lightly grease bottom and side of a 10-inch tube pan. Sprinkle with a little flour. Rotate to coat inside of pan evenly; shake out excess flour.

2 Sift flour on waxed paper. Gently spoon into a 1-cup measure; level off. Measure 3 cups flour in all. Turn back into sifter, along with baking powder and ¼ teaspoon salt.

3 Sift all together onto waxed paper; set aside. With mixer at high speed, beat egg whites with ¼ teaspoon salt till foamy throughout. Beat in 1 cup sugar, ¼ cup at a time,

4 beating well after each addition. Beat until soft peaks form when beater is slowly raised. On foil or waxed paper, grate orange and lemon peels on fine grater; measure.

5 In large bowl, at high speed, with same beater (don't wash), beat butter with remaining cup of sugar until light and fluffy—5 minutes. Beat in yolks until light and fluffy.

6 At high speed, beat in peels, lemon juice, and 2 tablespoons water until smooth. Divide flour mixture into thirds; at low speed, blend in, ⅓ at a time, just until combined—

7 takes about 1 minute. At low speed, blend in egg whites, half at a time, just until blended, scraping bowl and guiding batter into the beater. (Be sure not to overmix.)

8 Turn batter into prepared pan, cleaning bowl with rubber scraper. Bake, in middle of oven, 60 minutes, or until cake tester inserted in center of cake comes out clean.

9 Cool on rack 15 minutes. Gently loosen sides with spatula; turn out; cool. To glaze: Blend butter, sugar, lemon juice, peel until smooth. Then drizzle over cake.

CHEF'S TIPS

Cake making is an exacting art; read the recipe through completely before starting. Ingredients must be measured accurately; use standardized measuring cups and spoons. For dry ingredients, use metal cups (set of ¼-, ⅓-, ½-, and 1-cup), and heap the cup or spoon to overflowing; then level off excess with a spatula. For liquids, use a standard glass measuring cup, with lip, marked off in quarters and thirds. Place cup on flat surface; measure at eye level.

When recipe calls for sifted flour, sift before measuring (even though flour may be labeled "presifted"). Never pack down flour in cup.

Do not make substitutions in ingredients. Always use the size and type of pan called for. For this cake, you may use a regular 10-inch tube pan or one with a removable bottom. If you use a pan with a nonstick coating, follow the manufacturer's directions.

Separate eggs while they are cold from the refrigerator. Have other ingredients at room temperature. Let butter or margarine stand at room temperature to soften slightly.

Let cake cool completely before storing, wrapped in foil, in refrigerator.

To serve: Slice cake thinly, using a knife with a thin, sharp edge, not serrated. If serving cake unglazed, sift a little confectioners' sugar over top. You may store this cake, unglazed and wrapped in foil, in the freezer for several months.

FRUITCAKE TO FIT YOUR FAMILY

TO PREPARE PANS FOR FRUITCAKES:

Pans should be lightly greased with oil or shortening, then lined with heavy brown paper, cut to fit pan and lightly greased. For cupcakes, use ungreased, 2¼-inch cupcake liners in ungreased muffin-pan cups.

FRUITCAKE GLAZE

⅓ cup light corn syrup
1 tablespoon lemon juice

1. In small saucepan, combine corn syrup and lemon juice with 1 table-spoon water.
2. Bring to boiling; reduce heat, and simmer, stirring, 5 minutes, or until mixture is reduced to ⅓ cup. Let cool completely.
3. Use glaze to brush surface of fruitcake. Decorate with nuts and candied fruits.

FRUITCAKE FROSTING

1½ cups unsifted confectioners' sugar
2 tablespoons light cream
1 teaspoon vanilla extract

1. In small bowl, combine sugar, cream, and vanilla; beat until smooth. Spread top of cake with frosting, letting it run down side.
2. Decorate fruitcake with nuts and candied fruits.

BAKING CHART FOR FRUITCAKES

Pan Size	Amount of Batter	Baking Time	Yield
10-by-4-inch tube pan	1 recipe (13 cups batter)	3 hours at 275F	1 large tube cake
8½-by-4½-by-2½-inch loaf pan	1 recipe (5 cups batter per pan)	2 hours at 275F	2 (8½-inch) loaf cakes: use leftover batter to make another size
4½-by-3-by-2-inch loaf pan	1 recipe (1½ cups batter per pan)	1½ hours at 300F	8 (4½-inch) loaf cakes; use leftover batter to make cupcakes
1-lb shortening can	1 recipe (1¾ cups batter per pan)	1¾ hours at 300F	6 cakes; use leftover batter to make cupcakes
2½-inch muffin-pan cups	¼ cup for each cupcake	1 hour at 300F	About 56 cupcakes

GEORGE RATKAI

They're all made from the same batter, laden with fruits and nuts and moist with sherry. But you can make fruitcake in many sizes: large for a family, small for a couple, or just bite-size. The latter can be served in paper frills, like French pastry, or wrapped in foil and attached to a gift. Better start now: For flavors to blend and mellow, fruitcake takes time.

1 Day before: In large plastic container or kettle, combine fruits, nuts, and ½ cup sherry; mix well, using a large wooden spoon or with hands. Let stand, covered, overnight at room temperature. Next day, prepare pan. Make cake batter: Sift flour with baking powder, salt, and nutmeg. In large bowl, with electric

2 mixer at high speed, beat butter, sugar, and vanilla until smooth. Beat in eggs, one at a time, beating after each addition; continue beating until very light and fluffy. At low speed, beat in flour mixture just to combine. Preheat oven to 275F. Add batter to fruit mixture; mix with large wooden spoon or with hands until well combined.

3 Turn into pan, packing lightly; smooth with rubber scraper. (Bite-size shown at left.) Bake 3 hours, or until cake tester inserted in center comes out clean. Cool completely in pan on wire rack. Loosen edge with spatula; turn out of pan; peel off paper. Soak a large square of cheesecloth in ⅓ cup sherry. Wrap cake in the cheesecloth;

4 then wrap tightly in foil. Store in refrigerator or in an airtight container in a cool place. Resoak cheesecloth with sherry as it dries out—about once a week. Store cake 3 to 4 weeks to develop flavor. To serve: Frost or glaze cake, and decorate with candied fruit and nuts, as pictured. Makes a 10-inch, round, 7-pound cake.

INGREDIENTS

1 cup candied whole red and green cherries
½ cup cubed candied pineapple
2 cups watermelon pickle, drained and cut into ½-inch pieces
½ cup diced candied lemon peel
1 pkg (15 oz) raisins
1 can (8 oz) walnuts
1 can (6 oz) pecan halves
1 can (4 oz) slivered almonds
1 cup hazelnuts

Sherry
CAKE BATTER
3 cups unsifted all-purpose flour
½ teaspoon baking powder
½ teaspoon salt
½ teaspoon nutmeg
1 cup butter or regular margarine, softened
2 cups sugar
1 teaspoon vanilla extract
6 eggs

A CAKE FOR ALL THE SEASON

The holidays are on the way, and here's a festive cake you can serve all through the season. It's a light fruitcake, studded with raisins, nuts and cherries and mellowed in bourbon, Southern style. Slice thinly and serve with coffee, sherry or even eggnog. It keeps well for weeks, and costs less than most fruitcakes.

1 Preheat oven to 350F. Grease and flour well a 10-inch kuchen, bundt or tube pan. In large bowl, combine walnuts, cherries and raisins with ½ cup bourbon; mix well. Let stand at room temperature several hours or overnight—liquid will be absorbed.

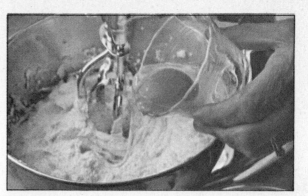

2 On sheet of waxed paper, sift flour with baking powder, salt and nutmeg; set aside. In large bowl of electric mixer, at medium speed, beat butter, sugar and vanilla until smooth and light and fluffy. Add eggs, one at a time, beating well after each addition.

3 Beat at medium speed 4 minutes, occasionally scraping side of bowl and guiding batter into beaters with rubber scraper. Batter will become thick and fluffy and lighter in color. At low speed, gradually beat in flour mixture until smooth.

4 Add to fruit; mix with wooden spoon to combine well. Turn into prepared pan; smooth top with spatula. Bake in center of oven 1 hour and 20 minutes in kuchen pan; 1 hour and 15 minutes in bundt pan; 1 hour and 10 minutes in tube pan.

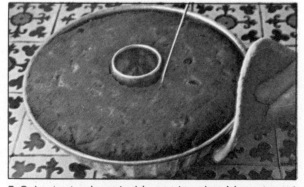

5 Cake tester inserted in center should come out clean. Cool in pan on wire rack 20 minutes. Use small spatula to loosen cake around inside; invert on wire rack; cool completely. In small bowl, soak a large piece of cheesecloth in ½ cup bourbon.

6 Stretch cheesecloth on large piece of foil. Place cake in center. Wrap cake in cheesecloth; then wrap in foil. Refrigerate several days to mellow. (Will keep several weeks in refrigerator.) To serve, slice thinly; let warm to room temperature.

WALNUT-RAISIN CAKE

2 cups chopped walnuts or pecans
1 jar (3½ oz) candied red cherries, quartered
2 cups light or dark raisins

½ cup bourbon
3½ cups sifted all-purpose flour (sift before measuring)
1½ teaspoons baking powder
½ teaspoon salt
1 teaspoon nutmeg

1½ cups butter or regular margarine, softened
2 cups sugar
1 teaspoon vanilla extract
7 eggs
½ cup bourbon

A MAGNIFICENT FRENCH DESSERT

Baba au rhum, that glorious yeast cake baked with raisins and citron, soaked in rum syrup and gleaming with apricot glaze, is one of the great desserts of French *haute cuisine.* To add it to your repertoire, see the directions on the following page. Serve with whipped cream.

1. Grease a 10-by-4-inch tube pan. Check temperature of water with thermometer. Sprinkle yeast over water in electric-mixer bowl; stir to dissolve. Add ¼ cup sugar, the salt, eggs and 2¼ cups flour. At medium speed, beat 4 minutes, or until smooth.

2 While beating, scrape side of bowl and guide mixture into beater with rubber scraper. Add butter; beat 2 minutes, or until well blended. At low speed, beat in rest of flour until smooth—2 minutes. Stir in the citron and currants; mix well. Batter will be thick.

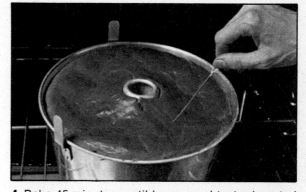

3 Turn into tube pan; spread evenly. Cover with towel. Let rise in warm place (85F), free from drafts, about 1 hour and 10 minutes, or until dough has risen to ½ inch from top. Preheat oven to 400F. Place pan on oven rack; do not jar or baba may fall.

4 Bake 45 minutes, until brown and tester inserted comes out clean. Make syrup: In pan, combine sugar and 2 cups water; bring to boil; stir to dissolve. Boil, uncovered, 10 minutes; reduce heat. Add fruit; simmer 10 minutes. Remove from heat; add rum.

5 With spatula, loosen side of baba from pan. Turn out of pan onto rack; cool 15 minutes. Return baba to pan; place on cookie sheet. Gradually pour hot syrup, with fruit slices, over baba. Continue until all syrup is absorbed. Let stand 2 hours or longer.

6 Meanwhile, make glaze: Over low heat, melt preserves. Stir in the lemon juice; strain. Refrigerate ½ hour. To serve: Turn baba out on platter. Arrange fruit slices on top, as pictured. Brush with glaze. If desired, serve with whipped cream. Serves 12.

BABA AU RHUM

¾ cup warm water (105 to 115F)
2 pkg active dry yeast
¼ cup sugar
1 teaspoon salt
6 eggs
3¾ cups sifted*
all-purpose flour
*Sift before measuring.

¾ cup butter, softened
½ cup finely chopped citron
or grated orange peel
¼ cup currants or seedless
raisins

RUM SYRUP
2½ cups sugar

1 unpeeled, medium-size orange,
sliced crosswise
½ unpeeled lemon, sliced
1 to 1½ cups light rum

APRICOT GLAZE
1 cup apricot preserves
2 teaspoons lemon juice

One of the delights of summer in Germany is fruit kuchen, an open-face, fresh-fruit pie served warm from the oven. It's made with pastry crust or raised yeast-dough crust; a custard mixture is poured over the fruit before baking. We've used fresh ripe peaches for our version, plus a crispy, rich biscuit crust, somewhat like shortcake. Kuchen can also be made with canned or frozen fruit.

Fragrant peach kuchen is especially delicious with whipped cream or à la mode. Time the kuchen to bake during dinner so that it will be at just the right temperature to serve for dessert. The batter may be mixed ahead of time, turned into a baking pan and refrigerated for as long as 3 hours. At brunch, serve kuchen instead of coffeecake.

What's Kuchen?
Peach Kuchen!

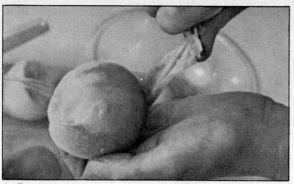

1 Pour enough boiling water over peaches in large bowl to cover. Let stand 1 minute to loosen skins; then drain, and plunge into cold water for a few seconds to prevent softening of fruit. With paring knife, pare peaches; place in large bowl.

2 Preheat oven to 400F. Sprinkle peaches with lemon juice to prevent darkening. Slice into the bowl; toss to coat with lemon juice; set aside. Onto sheet of waxed paper, sift flour with the sugar, baking powder, and salt. In large mixing

3 bowl, using fork, beat eggs with milk and lemon peel. Add flour mixture and melted butter, mixing with fork until smooth—1 minute. Do not overmix. Butter a 9-inch springform pan, pictured, or a 9-inch round layer-cake pan. (If

4 cake pan is used, kuchen must be served from pan.) Turn batter into pan; spread evenly over bottom. (At this point, kuchen may be refrigerated several hours, or until about ½ hour before baking.) Combine sugar and cinnamon; mix well.

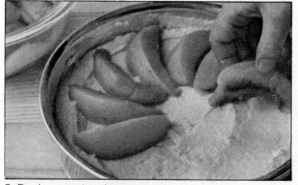

5 Drain peach slices; arrange on batter, around edge of pan, as pictured; fill in center with 5 peach slices. Sprinkle evenly with sugar-cinnamon mixture. Bake 25 minutes. Remove kuchen from oven. With a fork, beat egg yolk with cream.

6 Pour over peaches. Bake 10 minutes longer. Cool 10 minutes on wire rack. To serve, remove side of springform pan. Serve kuchen warm, cut into wedges, with sweetened whipped cream or soft vanilla ice cream. Makes 8 to 10 servings.

FRESH PEACH KUCHEN

Boiling water
2 lb ripe peaches, peeled
and sliced (about 6); or
2½ pkg (10-oz size) frozen
sliced peaches, drained
2 tablespoons lemon juice
KUCHEN BATTER
1½ cups sifted
all-purpose flour

½ cup sugar
2 teaspoons baking powder
½ teaspoon salt
2 eggs
2 tablespoons milk
1½ tablespoons grated
lemon peel
¼ cup butter or regular
margarine, melted

TOPPING
¼ cup sugar
½ teaspoon ground
cinnamon
1 egg yolk
3 tablespoons heavy cream

Sweetened whipped cream
or soft vanilla ice cream

A SPECIAL SUMMER DESSERT

Fresh-fruit kuchen is Europe's answer to our shortcake. A layer of biscuit dough is covered with slices of cinnamon-sprinkled fruit. We chose plums; you could also use peaches, green apples or alternating layers of all three. Serve warm from the oven with whipped cream, custard or cinnamon ice-cream sauce—or, for breakfast, all by itself. Step-by-step directions on the next page.

1 Grease a 13-by-9-by-2-inch baking pan or dish. Wash plums; drain. For easier slicing, cut each plum in half; then cut each half into 4 slices to measure 4½ cups. (If using apples, pare, quarter, core and slice thinly; measure 3 cups.) Preheat oven to 400F.

2 Into medium bowl, sift flour with ¼ cup sugar, the baking powder and salt. With fork or pastry blender, cut in ¼ cup butter until mixture resembles coarse crumbs. In small bowl, beat egg slightly with fork; then add milk and vanilla, blending well with fork.

3 Add to flour mixture, beating vigorously with fork until smooth—about 1 minute; batter will be quite stiff. Using spatula or rubber scraper, spread batter evenly over bottom of prepared pan. Arrange plum slices over batter, to cover completely, as shown.

4 Place thin sides down, slightly overlapping, in five parallel rows. Place any extra slices between rows. Topping: Mix ¼ cup sugar, 1 teaspoon cinnamon and the melted butter. Spoon over fruit. Bake 35 minutes, or until fruit is tender and pastry is golden.

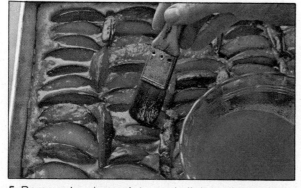

5 Remove to wire rack to cool slightly. (Meanwhile, remove ice cream from freezer to soften.) In small skillet, over medium heat, mix preserves with 1 tablespoon water, stirring until melted. Brush over plums. Cut between rows of fruit into 10 rectangles.

6 Serve warm with whipped cream or Cinnamon Ice-Cream Sauce. Sauce: In medium bowl, combine softened ice cream, sugar and cinnamon; mix well with wooden spoon until smooth. Turn into chilled serving dish. Freeze if not using at once. Serves 10.

FRESH PLUM KUCHEN

2 lb plums or 1½ lb tart apples
1¼ cups all-purpose flour
(sifted before measuring)
¼ cup sugar
1½ teaspoons baking powder
½ teaspoon salt
¼ cup butter or regular margarine

1 egg, ¼ cup milk
1 teaspoon vanilla extract
TOPPING
¼ cup sugar
1 teaspoon ground cinnamon
¼ cup butter or margarine,
melted

⅓ cup strawberry preserves
Whipped cream or
CINNAMON ICE-CREAM SAUCE
1 quart vanilla
ice cream
1 tablespoon sugar
2 teaspoons ground cinnamon

MOST LIKELY TO SUCCEED

GEORGE RATKAI

1 Preheat oven to 425F. Wash berries in cold water; drain. Set aside several nice ones for garnish. Remove hulls from rest of berries; slice half of berries into bowl; toss with ¼ cup granulated sugar. With fork crush other half of berries with ¼ cup sugar.

2 With portable electric mixer, beat cream with confectioners' sugar just until stiff; refrigerate. Lightly grease an 8-by-1½-inch round layer-cake pan. With sifter placed in medium bowl, sift flour with ¼ cup granulated sugar, the baking powder and salt.

3 With pastry blender, or two knives used scissors fashion, cut ½ cup butter into flour mixture until it is in very small particles, each coated with flour (resembles small peas). Break egg into a 1-cup measuring cup. Add milk to measure ¾ cup. Mix with fork.

4 Make well in center of flour mixture. Pour in milk-egg mixture all at once; mix vigorously with fork until moistened. Turn into prepared pan, scraping bowl with rubber scraper. With the rubber scraper, smooth top of dough so that it is even in pan.

5 Bake 25 to 30 minutes, or until golden and cake tester inserted in center comes out clean. Loosen edge with sharp knife; turn out on a wire rack. Using a long, serrated knife, cut cake in half crosswise. Place bottom of cake, cut side up, on serving plate.

6 Brush surface with melted butter. Spoon on half of crushed and sliced berries; set top in place, cut side down. Spoon on rest of berries. Mound whipped cream lightly in center. Garnish with whole berries, as shown. Serve warm, in wedges. Serves 9.

OLD-FASHIONED STRAWBERRY SHORTCAKE

TOPPING
2 pint boxes fresh strawberries
½ cup granulated sugar
1 cup heavy cream
2 tablespoons confectioners'
sugar

SHORTCAKE
2 cups sifted all-purpose
flour (sift before measuring)
¼ cup granulated sugar
3 teaspoons baking powder
½ teaspoon salt

½ cup butter or regular
margarine, cut into chunks
1 egg
Milk
2 tablespoons butter or
margarine, melted

1 Preheat oven to 350F. Drain pineapple slices, reserving 2 tablespoons of the syrup. In a very heavy or iron, 10-inch skillet with heat-resistant handle, melt butter over medium heat. Add brown sugar, stirring until sugar is melted. Remove from heat.

2 Arrange 8 pineapple slices on sugar mixture, overlapping slices slightly around edge of pan. Put one slice in center. Fill centers with pecan halves. Halve three remaining pineapple slices. Arrange around inside edge of skillet. Put pecans in centers.

3 Into medium bowl, sift flour with granulated sugar, baking powder and salt. Add shortening and milk. With electric mixer at high speed, beat 2 minutes, or until mixture is smooth. Add egg and reserved 2 tablespoons pineapple syrup; beat 2 minutes longer.

4 Gently pour cake batter over pineapple in skillet, spreading evenly, being careful not to disarrange pineapple. On rack in center of oven, bake 40 to 45 minutes, or until golden in color and surface of cake springs back when it's gently pressed with fingertip.

5 Let skillet stand on wire rack 5 minutes to cool just slightly. With rotary beater, beat cream until stiff. With small spatula, loosen cake from edge of skillet all around. Place serving platter over the cake, and turn upside down; shake gently; lift off skillet.

6 Serve cake warm, with the whipped cream or ice cream. *Note:* The pineapple upside-down cake was traditionally baked in an iron skillet. If your skillet does not have an iron or heatproof handle, wrap handle in foil before placing in the oven. Serves 8.

OLD-FASHIONED PINEAPPLE UPSIDE-DOWN CAKE (See page 124 for illustration.)

3 cans (8¼-oz size) sliced pineapple in heavy syrup (12 slices)
¼ cup butter or margarine
⅔ cup light brown sugar, packed

⅓ cup pecan halves
1 cup unsifted all-purpose flour
¾ cup granulated sugar
1½ teaspoons baking powder
½ teaspoon salt

¼ cup shortening
½ cup milk
1 egg
1 cup heavy cream, chilled, or 1 pint vanilla ice cream

1 Crepe batter: In medium bowl, combine flour, oil, eggs, egg yolks and ½ cup milk; beat with rotary beater until smooth. Add rest of milk, beating until blended and smooth. Refrigerate, covered, for 2 hours or longer (overnight is better).

2 Orange sauce: In medium skillet, melt ¼ cup butter. Stir in ⅓ cup sugar, shredded orange peel and juice; cook over low heat, stirring occasionally, until peel is translucent—10 minutes. Add oranges and ¼ cup Grand Marnier or Cointreau.

3 Crepes: Slowly heat a 7-inch skillet until a drop of water sizzles and rolls off. For each crepe, brush skillet lightly with butter. Pour in 2 tablespoons batter, rotating pan to cover bottom of skillet evenly. Cook until lightly browned. Turn; brown slightly.

4 Cool on rack; stack with waxed paper between. Orange butter: In small bowl, with electric beater, cream sweet butter with sugar until fluffy. Blend in Grand Marnier and orange peel. Use to spread on crepes—about 1 tablespoon for each one.

5 Fold each in half, then in half again. Arrange in pattern in orange sauce in chafing dish or skillet; cook over low heat just until sauce is hot and crepes are heated through. (Crepes and sauce may be made ahead and refrigerated separately.)

6 To serve flaming: Bring crepes to table right in chafing dish or skillet. Gently heat brandy in small saucepan just until vapor rises, no longer. Ignite with match and pour flaming brandy over heated crepes. Serve with sauce. Makes 6 to 8 servings.

CREPES SUZETTE (See page 18 for illustration.)

CREPES
1 cup unsifted all-purpose flour
¼ cup salad oil
2 eggs, 2 egg yolks
1½ cups milk

ORANGE SAUCE
¼ cup sweet butter
⅓ cup sugar
1 tablespoon coarsely shredded orange peel
⅓ cup orange juice
1 cup orange sections
¼ cup Grand Marnier or Cointreau

Butter or margarine

ORANGE BUTTER
¾ cup sweet butter
½ cup sugar
⅓ cup Grand Marnier or Cointreau
¼ cup grated orange peel

¼ cup brandy

THE ULTIMATE CHEESECAKE

One of New York's most famous restaurants was Lindy's; it was jammed night after night with Broadway's brightest stars, but the main attraction was its famous cheesecake. Though Lindy's is gone now, you can still enjoy what many think is the greatest cheesecake ever made. Serve it glazed with pineapple, un-glazed, or with sour cream spread thick and smooth on top. With only a few minor changes, our recipe is just like the one used at Lindy's. You'll find the same crisp cookie crust and the daringly rich cream-cheese filling, touched with just a hint of lemon.

1 Preheat oven to 400F. Grease inside of 9-inch springform pan (3 inches high). Remove side. Make crust: In medium bowl, combine flour, sugar, lemon peel, vanilla. Make well in center; with fork, blend in yolk and butter. Mix with fingertips until smooth.

2 On bottom of pan, form half of dough into ball. Place waxed paper on top; roll pastry to edge of pan. Remove paper. Bake 6 to 8 minutes, or until golden. Cool. Meanwhile, divide rest of dough into three parts. Cut six strips of waxed paper, 3 inches wide.

3 On dampened surface, between paper strips, roll each part 2¼ inches wide and 9 inches long. Assemble springform pan with crust on bottom. Line inside of pan with pastry strips, overlapping ends. Remove waxed-paper strips. Preheat oven to **500.**

4 Filling: In large mixer bowl, blend cheese, sugar, flour, peels and vanilla at high speed. Beat in eggs and yolks, one at a time; beat until smooth, occasionally scraping bowl with spatula. Beat in cream. Pour into pan. Bake 10 minutes. Lower oven to 250F.

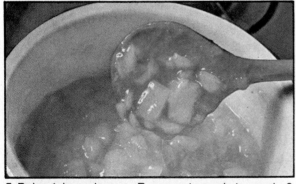

5 Bake 1 hour longer. Remove to rack to cool—2 hours. Make glaze: In small saucepan, combine sugar and cornstarch. Stir in remaining ingredients. Over medium heat, bring to boiling, stirring; boil 1 minute, or until thickened and translucent. Cool.

6 Spread surface of cheesecake with glaze; refrigerate until well chilled—3 hours or overnight. To serve: Loosen pastry from side of pan with spatula. Remove side of springform pan. Garnish with sliced strawberries, if desired. Cut into wedges. Serves 16.

CHEESECAKE

CRUST:
1 cup sifted all-purpose flour
(sift before measuring)
¼ cup sugar
1 teaspoon grated lemon peel
½ teaspoon vanilla extract
1 egg yolk
¼ cup butter or regular margarine,
softened

FILLING:
5 pkg (8-oz size) cream cheese,
softened
1¾ cups sugar
3 tablespoons flour
2 teaspoons grated lemon peel
1½ teaspoons grated orange peel
¼ teaspoon vanilla extract
5 eggs, plus 2 egg yolks

¼ cup heavy cream

PINEAPPLE GLAZE:
2 tablespoons sugar
4 teaspoons cornstarch
2 cans (8¼-oz size) crushed
pineapple in heavy syrup, undrained
2 tablespoons lemon juice
2 drops yellow food color

COLD POWER COOKING

STRAWBERRY AND CREAM CHEESECAKE

GRAHAM-CRACKER CRUST:

1 cup graham-cracker crumbs, 2 tablespoons sugar
⅓ cup butter or regular margarine, melted

CHEESE FILLING:

2 env unflavored gelatine
¾ cup sugar, ¼ teaspoon salt
3 egg yolks, 1 cup milk
3 pkg(8-oz size) cream cheese (at room temperature)
2 tablespoons grated lemon peel
2 tablespoons lemon juice
1 teaspoon vanilla extract

3 egg whites (at room temperature), ¼ cup sugar
1 cup (8-oz) sour cream

GLAZE:

½ cup sugar
1 tablespoon cornstarch
2 pints fresh strawberries, washed and hulled

1 Make Graham-Cracker Crust: In small bowl, combine crumbs, 2 tablespoons sugar, and the butter; mix well with fork. Reserve ¼ cup. With back of spoon, press rest of mixture on bottom of a 9-inch springform pan. Refrigerate. Make Filling: In small, heavy saucepan, combine gelatine, ¾ cup sugar, and the salt. In small bowl, with wire whisk, beat egg yolks with milk until smooth; gradually stir into gelatine mixture; mix well. Cook

2 over medium heat, stirring until gelatine is dissolved and custard is thickened slightly (should form coating on metal spoon)—about 5 minutes. Remove from heat; cool 10 minutes. In large bowl, with electric mixer, at medium speed, beat cream cheese, lemon peel, lemon juice, and vanilla until smooth—3 minutes. Slowly add cooled custard, beating at low speed just to blend. Set in a bowl of ice water to chill, stirring occasionally, until

3 mixture mounds (partially set) when lifted with spoon. Meanwhile, at medium speed and using clean beaters, beat egg whites until soft peaks form when beater is slowly raised. Gradually add ¼ cup sugar, beating until stiff peaks form. Add beaten egg whites and the sour cream to cheese mixture; beat at low speed just until smooth. Turn into the prepared pan, spreading evenly. Refrigerate until firm and well chilled—at least 4 hours

4 or overnight. Glaze 1 hour before serving: In small saucepan, combine sugar and cornstarch. With fork, crush 2 cups berries. Stir into sugar mixture with ¼ cup water. Bring to boiling, stirring, until thickened and translucent. Strain; cool. To serve, loosen side of pan with spatula; remove. Arrange some of berries over cake. Top with some of glaze. Sprinkle reserved crumbs around edge. Serve rest of berries in glaze. Serves 10 to 12.

NO-BAKING STRAWBERRY CHEESECAKE

This delicate summer cheesecake can be made a day ahead, refrigerated overnight, and glazed just before serving. Points to Remember: (1) To make your own graham-cracker crumbs, crush crackers with a rolling pin until very fine between two sheets of waxed paper. (2) Let cream cheese stand at room temperature 1 hour to soften—it's easier to combine, makes a smoother mixture. (3) For a deep cheesecake, use a springform pan so that sides can be removed while cake itself stands on the bottom of the pan. (4) For serving, cut with a sharp knife; lift up with a pie server. (5) In cooking the custard, use a heavy saucepan, and stir constantly, as custard scorches and eggs curdle easily. Otherwise, you're safer with a double boiler. (6) Gelatine must be totally dissolved. If it is not, cake may not be firm enough to cut.

McCall's Cooking School
GETTING THE FEEL OF PASTRY

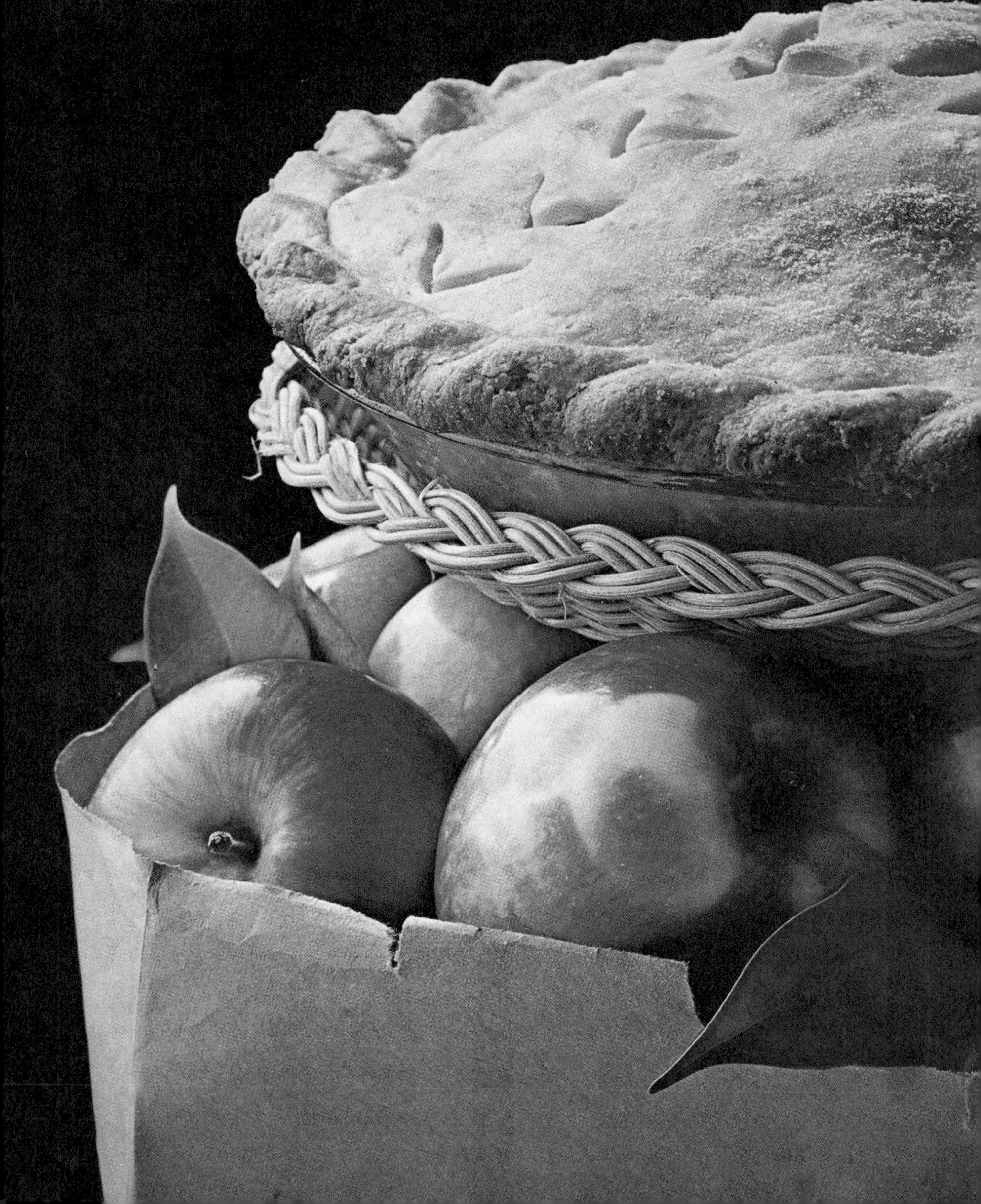

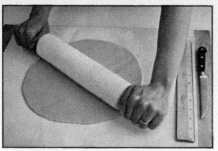

1 Make pastry as package directs. Handling gently, shape pastry into a ball. Divide in half; form each half into a round; then flatten each with palm of hand. On lightly floured pastry cloth (see Points, below), roll

2 out half of pastry into a 12-inch circle, using a ball-bearing rolling pin. Roll with light strokes from center to edge, lifting rolling pin as you reach edge. Place a 9-inch heat-resistant glass pie plate on pastry circle;

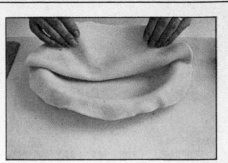

3 it should measure 1 inch wider all around. Fold rolled pastry in half; carefully transfer to pie plate, making sure fold is in center of pie plate. Unfold pastry, and fit carefully into pie plate, pressing gently with fingers, so

4 pastry fits snugly all around. Do not stretch pastry. Refrigerate until ready to use. Preheat oven to 425F. In small bowl, mix sugar, flour, cinnamon, nutmeg, and salt. In a large bowl, toss the apples with the lemon juice. Add

5 sugar mixture to sliced apples; toss lightly to combine. Roll out remaining pastry into 12-inch circle (as directed in Step 2). Fold over in quarters; cut slits for steam vents. Turn the apple mixture into pastry-lined pie plate,

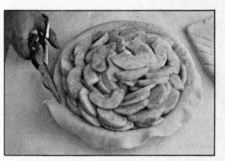

6 mounding up high in center. This supports top crust. Dot apples with butter cut in small pieces. Using scissors, trim overhanging edge of pastry so it measures ½ inch from rim of pie plate. Carefully place folded pastry

7 so that point is at the center of filling, and gently unfold. Using scissors, trim overhanging edge of pastry (for top crust), so it measures 1 inch from edge all around. Moisten the edge of the bottom pastry with a little water.

8 Fold top pastry under edge of bottom pastry. With fingers, press edge together to seal, so juices won't run out. Press upright to form a standing rim. Crimp edge: Place thumb on edge of pastry at an angle. Pinch dough

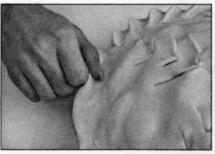

9 between index finger and thumb. Repeat at same angle all around pie. Bake 45 to 50 minutes, or until apples are fork-tender and crust is golden. Serve warm, using pie server, with ice cream or Cheddar cheese. Serves 8.

PERFECT APPLE PIE

1 pkg (9½- to 11-oz) piecrust mix 1 cup sugar 2 tablespoons flour 1 teaspoon cinnamon	⅛ teaspoon nutmeg ¼ teaspoon salt 7 cups thinly sliced, pared tart cooking apples (2½ lb)	2 tablespoons lemon juice 2 tablespoons butter or regular margarine Ice cream or Cheddar cheese

POINTS TO REMEMBER: Good pie apples are tart, firm, and juicy, such as Northern Spy, Greening, and McIntosh. In rolling pastry, it's best to use a pastry cloth. Rub flour well into cloth, and brush off excess, then roll rolling pin covered with a stockinette across cloth. This keeps pastry from sticking without picking up excess flour. Roll pastry from center out, using light strokes and alternating direction to form an even circle.

They're American as apple pie and a lot easier to make—especially if you use a piecrust mix. One of the best apples to use in dumplings is the Rome Beauty. (Northern Spy is equally good but not as widely available.) Apples are simply peeled and cored, then stuffed with a delicious mixture of sugar and cinnamon, butter, raisins and walnuts, wrapped in the crust and baked. Serve them hot, topped with fluffy hard sauce that melts into a creamy topping, or with vanilla ice cream.

OLD-FASHIONED APPLE DUMPLINGS

GEORGE RATKAI

1 Make pastry as package label directs. Form pastry into a flat, 8-inch round; wrap in waxed paper; refrigerate. In small bowl, combine 3 tablespoons butter, granulated sugar, raisins, walnuts and cinnamon; blend with fork. Core apples with corer.

2 Pare apples and brush with lemon juice. Using spoon, fill hollows with raisin-walnut mixture. Preheat oven to 425F. Grease well a shallow baking pan, 15½ by 10½ by 1 inch. On lightly floured pastry cloth or floured surface, divide pastry evenly into sixths.

3 Form each piece into a round ball. Flatten each piece; then roll out from center into an 8½-inch square. Trim edges, using pastry wheel for decorative edge. Save trimmings. Place an apple in center of each square; brush edges lightly with water.

4 Bring each corner of square to top of apple; pinch edges of pastry together firmly, to cover apple completely. Reroll trimmings ¼ inch thick. With knife, cut out 24 leaves, 1¾ inches long and ¾ inch wide. Brush one end of each leaf lightly with water.

5 Press leaves on top of dumplings; put clove in center. Arrange in pan. Brush with yolk mixed with 1 tablespoon water. Bake, brushing once with juices in pan, 40 minutes, or until pastry is browned and apples are tender when tested with a wooden pick.

6 With broad spatula, remove dumplings to serving dishes. Serve warm, topped with Hard Sauce: In medium bowl, using portable electric beater, cream butter until light. At low speed, add vanilla and confectioners' sugar; beat until smooth. Serves 6.

APPLE DUMPLINGS WITH HARD SAUCE

1½ pkg (9½-to-11-oz size)
piecrust mix
3 tablespoons butter or
margarine, softened
3 tablespoons granulated sugar
1 tablespoon dark raisins
2 tablespoons chopped walnuts

¾ teaspoon ground cinnamon
6 large baking apples
(4 lb) —Rome Beauty,
Northern Spy
2 tablespoons lemon juice
Whole cloves
1 egg yolk

HARD SAUCE
½ cup butter or regular
margarine, softened
1 teaspoon vanilla extract
1¼ cups unsifted confectioners'
sugar

PICTURE-PERFECT PIE

Summer is the season for fresh fruit—and fresh-fruit pie. For this one we have combined two of the season's best—both relatively inexpensive and plentiful right now: sweet peaches and tart blueberries. Blended with tapioca, sugar and lemon and baked in our own flaky pastry, they make a dessert as delicious as it is beautiful. Piecrust is tricky but not if you follow the directions on the next page carefully.

GEORGE RATKAI

1 Sift flour with salt into medium bowl. With pastry blender, using short, cutting motion, cut in shortening to resemble coarse cornmeal. Sprinkle with ice water, 1 tablespoon at a time, tossing with fork after each addition. Push dampened part aside.

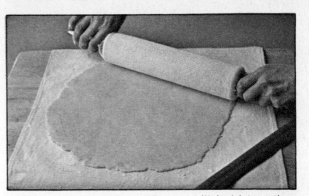

2 Sprinkle dry portion. (Pastry will hold together but not be sticky.) Shape into ball; refrigerate in waxed paper. Cut in half; flatten one half with palm of hand. On lightly floured surface, roll to an 11-inch circle; use light strokes from center to edge.

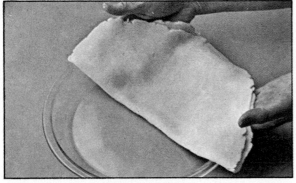

3 As you roll, alternate directions to shape even circle. Fold rolled pastry in half; carefully transfer to 9-inch pie plate, making sure fold is in center. Unfold pastry; fit down into pie plate—do not stretch. With knife, trim edge even with edge of pie plate.

4 Roll other half to an 11-inch circle. Fold in half; make several gashes near center for vents. Sprinkle lemon juice over fruit in large bowl. Mix sugar, tapioca and salt; toss lightly with fruit. Let stand 15 minutes. Turn into pastry, mounding in center.

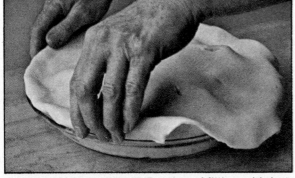

5 Preheat oven to 425F. Dot top of filling with butter. Carefully place pastry on top of filling, making sure fold is in center; unfold. Trim top crust ½ inch beyond edge of pie plate. Fold top crust under bottom crust and press together gently, to seal.

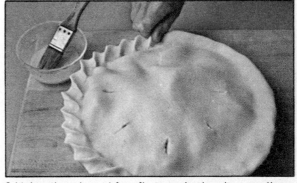

6 Using thumb and forefinger, pinch edge on diagonal all around. Brush top with egg yolk beaten with 1 tablespoon water. Bake 45 to 50 minutes, or until fruit is tender and crust is golden-brown. Cool partially on rack; serve warm. Serves 8.

PEACH-AND-BLUEBERRY PIE

PASTRY FOR 2-CRUST PIE
2 cups sifted all-purpose
flour (sift before measuring)
1 teaspoon salt
¾ cup shortening
4 tablespoons ice water

FILLING
2 tablespoons lemon juice
3 cups sliced, pitted,
peeled peaches (2¼ lb)
1 cup blueberries
1 cup sugar

2 tablespoons quick-cooking
tapioca
½ teaspoon salt
2 tablespoons butter or
margarine
1 egg yolk

For the flakiest pastry, handle very gently: Roll out, using as little flour as possible. Roll on a lightly floured pastry cloth with a rolling pin with stockinette, or roll between two sheets of lightly floured waxed paper.

COLD AND CREAMY— LEMON CHIFFON PIE

The tartness of lemon and the fluffy lightness of beaten egg whites combine to make lemon chiffon pie one of America's favorite desserts. Ours is a little different from traditional recipes— it's richer because we've added whipped cream to the basic filling, egg whites plus a soft custard made with egg yolks, lemon juice and gelatine. We've used a no-bake graham-cracker crust—the easiest kind to make. Instructions are on the following page.

1 Separate eggs, placing whites in large bowl of electric mixer, yolks in double-boiler top. Let whites warm to room temperature—about 1 hour. Make crust: Combine the crumbs, butter, ¼ cup sugar and the cinnamon in bowl; blend with fingers or fork.

2 With back of spoon, press mixture evenly on bottom and side, not on rim, of 9-inch pie plate. Refrigerate. Sprinkle gelatine over ¼ cup cold water to soften; set aside. With wooden spoon, beat yolks slightly. Stir in lemon juice, ½ cup sugar and the salt.

3 Cook, stirring, over hot, not boiling, water (water should not touch bottom of double boiler top) until mixture thickens and forms coating on a metal spoon —8 to 10 minutes. Add gelatine; stir to dissolve. Add lemon peel, 2 drops color. Remove from water.

4 Turn into medium bowl; set in a larger bowl of ice cubes to chill, stirring occasionally, until as thick as unbeaten egg white—10 minutes. Meanwhile, beat whites: At high speed, beat until soft peaks form when beater is slowly raised (peaks bend slightly).

5 Beat in ½ cup sugar, 2 tablespoons at a time, beating after each addition. Beat until stiff peaks form when beater is raised. With rotary beater, beat ½ cup cream until stiff. With wire whisk, gently fold gelatine mixture into whites just until combined.

6 Gently fold in whipped cream. Mound high in pie shell. Refrigerate until firm—3 hours. Beat ½ cup cream with 2 tablespoons confectioners' sugar until stiff. Turn into pastry bag with number-5 tip; make lattice on top, rosettes around edge. Serves 8.

LEMON CHIFFON PIE

4 eggs

GRAHAM-CRACKER CRUST
1¼ cups graham-cracker crumbs*
⅓ cup butter or regular margarine, softened

¼ cup granulated sugar
¼ teaspoon cinnamon

1 env unflavored gelatine
½ cup lemon juice
1 cup granulated sugar
¼ teaspoon salt

1 tablespoon grated lemon peel
Yellow food color
½ cup heavy cream

½ cup heavy cream
Confectioners' sugar

***To make crumbs: Crush about 18 graham crackers with rolling pin to make fine crumbs.**

THE SECRET OF PERFECT PUMPKIN PIE

Most pumpkin pies, even the best ones, wind up with soggy crusts. But not this one. There's a secret to making it that insures a light, flaky, melt-in-your-mouth crust every time: We bake the filling and the crust in separate pie pans. The filling itself is extra rich, made with heavy cream, five eggs, cinnamon, nutmeg and ginger. The eggs give it the delicate but firm consistency of custard, so it's easy, after the filling is baked, to slip it out of the baking dish and into the waiting crust. The bit of space between filling and crust is concealed with a decorative ribbon of whipped cream around the edge. Walnut halves top it off.

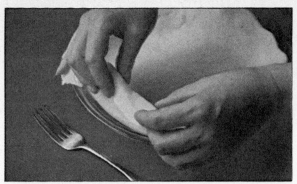

1 Make pastry: On lightly floured pastry cloth, with stockinette-covered rolling pin, roll three-fourths of pastry into 12-inch circle. Trim edge evenly. Fold pastry in half; lift to 9-inch pie plate, unfolding it carefully in pan. Fold edge under to build up all around.

2 Make scalloped edge: With fork, press edge of pastry flat, pinching each side of fork with fingers to form scallop (see above). Continue all around edge; then pinch each scallop again. Refrigerate pastry about 30 minutes. Meanwhile, preheat oven to 450F.

3 Prick entire surface of unbaked pie shell evenly with fork to prevent shell from puffing. Bake 10 to 12 minutes, or until golden. Cool completely on wire rack. Make filling: Set oven temperature at 350F. Butter inside of 9-inch pie plate. In large bowl,

4 combine filling ingredients. Beat with rotary beater until smooth. Pour 1½ cups filling into 2-cup measure. Pour rest of filling into buttered pie plate; set in large, shallow pan. Place in oven; add reserved filling. Pour water around pie plate to measure ½

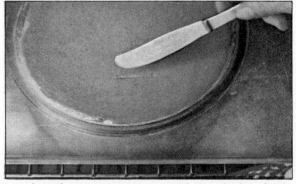

5 inch. Bake 50 minutes, or until tip of silver knife inserted near center comes out clean. Cool on wire rack. Loosen edge with spatula. Chill well—about 4 hours, or overnight. Several hours before serving, with spatula, loosen custard all around edge and

6 underneath, shaking to loosen. Holding custard above rim of pie shell, slip filling into shell. Decorate edge of pie, between filling and crust, with whipped cream in pastry bag with number-6 star tip. Then top with the walnut halves. Refrigerate. Makes 8 servings.

PUMPKIN PIE WITH A SECRET

1 pkg (10- or 11-oz size) piecrust mix	5 eggs (1⅓ cups)	1 cup heavy cream or canned evaporated milk, undiluted
1 tablespoon butter or margarine, softened	½ teaspoon cinnamon	
	½ teaspoon ginger	
	¼ teaspoon nutmeg	¾ cup heavy cream, well chilled, whipped with
PUMPKIN-CUSTARD FILLING	⅛ teaspoon cloves	2 tablespoons
¾ cup light-brown sugar, packed	½ teaspoon salt	confectioners' sugar
	1 can (1 lb) pumpkin (2 cups)	Walnut halves

"If you want to know how good a restaurant is," says a gentleman of our acquaintance, "order the chocolate mousse." This classic French dessert is meltingly rich and totally delectable. We think our version would win four stars for any restaurant, and it's surprisingly easy to make. For extra lightness, let the egg whites warm to room temperature before beating. Mousse can be stored for a day or two in the refrigerator, a week or two in the freezer without damaging its delicate texture. Instructions on next page.

MOUSSE AU CHOCOLAT

1 Make mousse a day or two ahead. Separate eggs, putting whites into a large bowl, yolks in a small one. Let whites warm to room temperature—1 hour. In top of double boiler, over hot, not boiling, water, melt semisweet chocolate with butter, stirring constantly.

2 Remove top of double boiler from water. With wooden spoon, beat in yolks, one at a time, beating well after each addition. Let cool 10 minutes; stir in Cognac. With portable mixer, beat whites until stiff, moist peaks form when beater is slowly raised.

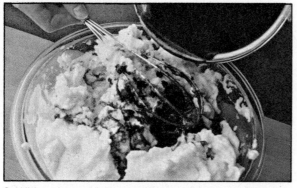

3 With wire whisk or rubber scraper, using an under-and-over motion, gently fold chocolate mixture into egg whites just enough to combine thoroughly; there should be no white streaks. Turn into an attractive, 1-quart serving dish. Refrigerate.

4 Several hours before serving, decorate mousse. To make chocolate curls, warm chocolate bar, still wrapped. Place in a warm spot just until soft, not melting. Then, with vegetable peeler pressing lightly, pare along bar in a long, thin stroke, to form a curl.

5 Make 8 curls. Lift with toothpick to plate; refrigerate. In small bowl, whip cream stiff. Turn into pastry bag with a number-6 star tip, pushing cream to end of bag. With tube held upright, squeeze whipped cream out in a 1-inch circle, twisting to form rosette.

6 Form about 8 whipped-cream rosettes around mousse, 1 inch from edge of bowl, with one large rosette in center. Using a toothpick, carefully place chocolate curls between rosettes, as pictured. Refrigerate until serving time. Makes 8 to 10 servings.

CHOCOLATE MOUSSE

8 eggs	10 tablespoons sweet or	1 bar (4 oz) milk chocolate
2 pkg (6-oz size) semisweet chocolate pieces	very lightly salted butter	¾ cup heavy cream
	¼ cup Cognac or brandy	

Note: The chocolate mousse may be made through Step 3, wrapped in foil and frozen for a week or two. To serve: Let thaw in refrigerator 4 to 5 hours; then decorate mousse, starting with Step 4.

Everybody's favorite Italian dessert is that sweet and creamy confection known as tortoni. It's basically a super-rich form of frozen mousse, made with sugar syrup, stiffly beaten egg white and whipped cream, flavored with almond extract and sprinkled with toasted almonds. Make it as the Italians do, in fluted paper cups (use the kind you bake cupcakes in); top with a maraschino cherry. Instructions, next page.

ITALIAN DELIGHT

1 Separate eggs: Crack shell; turn yolk from one half into the other, letting white run into small bowl, yolk into another. Turn each white into the small bowl of electric mixer as it is separated. (Take care that none of the yolk gets into the white.) Refrigerate yolks.

2 Let whites warm to room temperature—1 hour. Mix ¼ cup water with the sugar in 1-quart saucepan; stir over low heat to dissolve. Boil, uncovered, without stirring, to 236F on candy thermometer (syrup spins 2-inch thread when dropped from spoon).

3 Meanwhile, at high speed, beat whites with salt just until stiff peaks form when beater is slowly raised. Pour hot syrup in thin stream over whites; beat constantly until very stiff peaks form when beater is raised. Refrigerate, covered, 30 minutes.

4 Meanwhile, preheat oven to 350F. Place blanched almonds in shallow baking pan; bake just until lightly toasted—8 to 10 minutes. Chop almonds finely or grind finely in electric blender. Turn into small bowl. Stir in 1½ teaspoons almond extract. Set aside.

5 In medium bowl, beat cream, using portable electric mixer, with ¼ teaspoon almond extract and the vanilla until quite stiff. With wire whisk or rubber scraper, using an under-and-over motion, gently fold into egg-white mixture until well combined.

6 Spoon into 12 paper-lined, 2½-inch-size muffin-pan cups. Sprinkle with almond mixture; top with cherry. Cover with foil; freeze until firm—several hours or overnight. Makes 12. (For longer storage, remove from pan; wrap each well. Keeps 1 month.)

BISCUIT TORTONI

3 eggs	¼ cup whole blanched	1½ cups heavy cream
¾ cup sugar	almonds	¾ teaspoon vanilla extract
Dash salt	Almond extract	12 candied cherries

To make a fancy mold instead of individual desserts: In Step 6, turn the mixture into a 1-quart mold or bowl; cover with foil. Freeze until firm enough to unmold, or overnight. To unmold: Run a small spatula around the edge of mold; dip quickly into hot water; invert onto serving dish. Sprinkle with ground-almond mixture. Return to freezer until serving. Decorate with whipped cream and candied cherries. Makes 8 to 10 servings.

Old-fashioned caramel custard is one of the most delightful and healthful desserts you can serve your family. It's also one of the trickiest. As with any egg mixture, it demands careful handling. Our custard is made in a ring mold instead of individual cups, since this makes it easier both to prepare and to serve. Custard that is overcooked becomes watery and is not smooth. Our method is to place the mold in a pan of hot water while the custard is baking. There's a trick to caramelizing the sugar, too. It should be cooked over low heat just long enough to make a light-golden syrup. If cooked over high heat or too long, it develops a burned flavor. For an extra bit of drama, we've topped our custard with fresh fruit.

CARAMEL CUSTARD: HANDLE WITH CARE

1 Preheat oven to 325F. Sprinkle ½ cup sugar evenly over bottom of a small, heavy skillet (see picture 1). Cook slowly over very low heat, stirring occasionally with a wooden spoon, just until sugar melts to a golden syrup (picture 2). If the sugar is cooked too long

2 and at too high a temperature, it will be too dark and taste burned. Immediately pour syrup (picture 3) into bottom of 5-cup ring mold (8½ inches across and 2 inches deep). Tilt mold (picture 4), while syrup is still liquid, to coat bottom and side. (Caramel syrup will

3 harden.) Let cool. In large bowl, with wire whisk, beat eggs with sugar, salt and vanilla to mix well. Gradually add milk, beating until smooth, not frothy. Place prepared ring mold in shallow baking pan. Remove 1 cup egg mixture; reserve. Pour rest of mixture into mold.

4 Place baking pan on middle rack in oven; pour reserved mixture into mold (this eliminates spilling). Pour hot water into pan (picture 5) 1 inch deep around mold. Bake 55 to 60 minutes, or until a silver knife inserted 1 inch from edge comes out clean (picture 6).

5 Do not overbake; custard continues to bake after removal from oven. Remove mold from hot water to rack to cool completely; then refrigerate to chill —at least 1 hour. (Custard can be made day ahead.) The custard will settle slightly on cooling. To unmold:

6 Loosen edge with spatula. Place serving plate upside down on mold and reverse the two; shake gently to release; caramel will run down side. Toss fruit together lightly; use to fill center of custard. Spoon some of caramel sauce over each serving. Makes 6 to 8 servings.

CARAMEL CUSTARD

SYRUP
½cup granulated sugar

CUSTARD
5 eggs

½ cup granulated sugar
¼ teaspoon salt
1 teaspoon vanilla
extract
3½ cups milk

FRUIT FOR CENTER
½ pint fresh strawberries,
washed and hulled (1 cup)
1 cup drained pineapple cubes
½ lb seedless green grapes

A LUSCIOUS DESSERT

Cannoli are a traditional Sicilian dessert: crisp pastry shells filled with creamy ricotta cheese, whipped cream and bits of candied fruit. The extra-rich version pictured here is a specialty of TV's popular Italian cooking team, Margaret and Franco Romagnoli. The pastry is wrapped around cannoli forms (available in stores that carry European cooking ware) and deep-fried. Make them ahead; fill before serving.

1 Pastry: Place flour in a mound on pastry board. Make well in center; put in salt, sugar and dabs of soft butter. Add wine, and with fork stir in center. Keep stirring until most of flour is absorbed. You can work paste with your hands. Knead until smooth.

2 Almost all the remaining flour will have been picked up. Roll out no thicker than a noodle; cut into 3½-inch squares, if using 5-inch-long, 1-inch-diameter forms. Place forms diagonally on squares. Wrap pastry around form, one corner over the other.

3 Press corners together. If corners don't stick, moisten finger with water; apply to contact point and press again. Cover the bottom of the frying pan with about ¾ inch vegetable oil; heat to 375F. If you don't have a thermometer, drop in a bit of the dough.

4 If it immediately blisters and turns toast color, the temperature is right. Cannoli cook very fast and swell in size; three is a good number to cook at a time. Put them in the hot oil, turning carefully when one side is done. Remove from pan as soon as they are crisp.

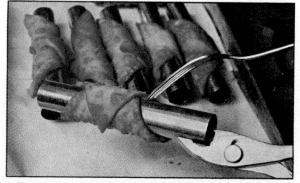

5 They should be a uniform toast color and rather blistered all around. Forms get hot; pointed pliers are best for lifting them out. Hold form with pliers; give a gentle push with fork to slip the fried cannoli off. Drain on paper towels. Put forms aside to cool.

6 When cooled, rewrap; continue frying. Using spatula or broad knife, fill cannoli first from one end and then the other. Press filling in gently to make sure centers are full. Scrape ends to smooth cream; dip ends in remaining candied fruit. Makes 16 to 18.

CANNOLI

FILLING
2 cups ricotta cheese
1 cup whipped heavy cream
3 tablespoons sugar
2 tablespoons candied fruit

1½ teaspoons vanilla extract

PASTRY
1 cup flour
¼ teaspoon salt

1 scant tablespoon sugar
1 tablespoon soft unsalted butter
¼ cup white wine
Vegetable oil for frying

For filling: Put ricotta in a bowl; fold in whipped cream, adding sugar as you fold. Chop candied fruit into tiny slivers; fold in all but a teaspoonful. Add vanilla. Refrigerate until shells are cooked and ready to be filled.

FILLED WITH SWEETNESS—AND LIGHT

Éclairs are a true luxury dessert—enticingly rich custard on the inside, soft, buttery pastry on the outside. They take various toppings: We chose creamy chocolate and powdered sugar. The dough, called pâte à choux, is basic to many cream-puff desserts. Be sure mixture is cool when you add the eggs; then beat vigorously for extra lightness and puff. Instructions are on next page.

1 Preheat oven to 400F. In medium saucepan, bring water, ⅓ cup butter and the salt to boiling. Remove from heat. Quickly add flour all at once. With wooden spoon, beat constantly over low heat until mixture forms ball and leaves side of pan. Remove from heat.

2 Using portable electric mixer or wooden spoon, beat in eggs, one at a time, beating very well after each addition. Continue beating vigorously until dough is shiny and satiny and breaks away in strands. Dough will be stiff and hold its shape.

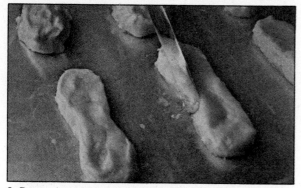

3 Drop dough by rounded tablespoons, 3 inches apart, on ungreased cookie sheet. With spatula, shape into 4-by-1½-inch strips, rounding ends and slightly indenting sides. Bake 35 to 40 minutes, or until puffed and golden. Cool on rack.

4 Filling: In small, heavy saucepan, heat 1½ cups milk until bubbling around edge. Mix sugar and cornstarch; stir, all at once, into hot milk. Over medium heat, cook, stirring, until bubbling. Reduce heat; simmer 1 minute. Beat a little of hot mixture into yolks.

5 Return to saucepan; cook, stirring, over medium heat until thickened. Add vanilla. Turn into bowl; refrigerate—with waxed paper on surface—1½ hours. Fold in cream. To fill: With sharp knife, cut off tops of éclairs crosswise. Remove some of soft dough inside.

6 Fill each with ¼ cup custard. Replace tops. Make glaze: In top of double boiler, over hot water, melt chocolate with butter. Blend in corn syrup and milk. Cool 5 minutes. Spoon over éclairs, placed on rack on tray. Serve at once or refrigerate. Makes 8.

ÉCLAIRS

¾ cup water
⅓ cup butter or regular margarine
⅛ teaspoon salt
¾ cup all-purpose flour (sift before measuring)
3 large eggs

CUSTARD FILLING
1½ cups milk
¼ cup sugar
1½ tablespoons cornstarch
2 egg yolks, slightly beaten
1 teaspoon vanilla extract
½ cup heavy cream, whipped

CHOCOLATE GLAZE
1 cup (6 oz) semisweet chocolate pieces
2 tablespoons butter or regular margarine
2 tablespoons corn syrup
3 tablespoons milk

Note: Or fill éclairs with sweetened whipped cream: Beat 1 cup chilled heavy cream with 3 tablespoons confectioners' sugar until stiff. Add 1 tablespoon vanilla extract. Fill éclairs; sprinkle tops with confectioners' sugar.